Caring for Your Adopted Child

An Essential Guide for Parents

Elaine E. Schulte, MD, MPH, FAAP ▪ Robin L. Michaelson

American Academy of Pediatrics
DEDICATED TO THE HEALTH OF ALL CHILDREN®

American Academy of Pediatrics Publishing Staff

Mary Lou White, *Chief Product and Services Officer/SVP, Membership, Marketing, and Publishing*

Mark Grimes, *Vice President, Publishing*

Kathryn Sparks, *Manager, Consumer Publishing*

Shannan Martin, *Production Manager, Consumer Publications*

Amanda Helmholz, *Medical Copy Editor*

Peg Mulcahy, *Manager, Art Direction and Production*

Sara Hoerdeman, *Marketing Manager, Consumer Products*

Published by the American Academy of Pediatrics
345 Park Blvd
Itasca, IL 60143
Telephone: 630/626-6000
Facsimile: 847/434-8000
www.aap.org

The American Academy of Pediatrics is an organization of 67,000 primary care pediatricians, pediatric medical subspecialists, and pediatric surgical specialists dedicated to the health, safety, and well-being of infants, children, adolescents, and young adults.

The information contained in this publication should not be used as a substitute for the medical care and advice of your pediatrician. There may be variations in treatment that your pediatrician may recommend based on individual facts and circumstances.

Statements and opinions expressed are those of the author and not necessarily those of the American Academy of Pediatrics.

Products and Web sites are mentioned for informational purposes only and do not imply an endorsement by the American Academy of Pediatrics (AAP). The AAP is not responsible for the content of external resources. Information was current at the time of publication.

Brand names are furnished for identification purposes only. No endorsement of the manufacturers or products mentioned is implied.

The publishers have made every effort to trace the copyright holders for borrowed materials. If they have inadvertently overlooked any, they will be pleased to make the necessary arrangements at the first opportunity.

This publication has been developed by the American Academy of Pediatrics. The contributors are expert authorities in the field of pediatrics. No commercial involvement of any kind has been solicited or accepted in development of the content of this publication. Disclosures: The authors report no disclosures.

Every effort is made to keep *Caring for Your Adopted Child: An Essential Guide for Parents* consistent with the most recent advice and information available from the American Academy of Pediatrics.

Special discounts are available for bulk purchases of this publication. E-mail Special Sales at aapsales@aap.org for more information.

Printed in the United States of America

9-405   1 2 3 4 5 6 7 8 9 10

CB0108

ISBN: 978-1-61002-215-6
eBook: 978-1-61002-216-3
EPUB: 978-1-61002-222-4
Kindle: 978-1-61002-223-1

Cover and publication designs by Peg Mulcahy

Library of Congress Control Number: 2017963218

What People Are Saying

Elaine Schulte and Robin Michaelson distill decades of professional and personal experiences into an accessible, encouraging summary of the joys—and challenges—of adoption. *Caring for Your Adopted Child* is a must-read guide for anyone considering, or underway with, adopting a child.

> — Lisa Damour, PhD, author of *Untangled: Guiding Teenage Girls Through the Seven Transitions into Adulthood*

&

As a pediatrician who has dedicated my career to serving adopted children and their families, this is a book that should've happened 25 years ago. Dr Schulte and Robin Michaelson have demonstrated a deep and passionate understanding of the evolving needs of adopted children. They've done an exceptional job speaking to parents in a way that's respectful and meaningful.

As adoptive parents and physicians, we bring a unique perspective to our work, and have been able to provide the specific anticipatory guidance that adoptive parents need. *Caring for Your Adopted Child* captures this guidance in words that are relatable for parents. This book will help ease the transition from pre-adoption to adoption, and throughout childhood, and celebrates the beauty of children and family.

Kudos to the American Academy of Pediatrics for providing this resource, and demonstrating their commitment, once again, to a specific population of children and families.

> — Jane Aronson, MD, FAAP, CEO and founder, Worldwide Orphans Foundation

&

As a pediatrician who cares for children and families formed through adoption, foster care, and kinship care, I am often asked the question, "Is this an adoption issue, or just a kid thing?" The answer most often is, "It's both." Children who come to their families through adoption have all of the same joys and struggles as other children, but these are often experienced through the lens of their lifelong adoption experiences. *Caring for Your Adopted Child* is an important addition to parenting literature, closing the gap between "regular" child-rearing books and "adoption" parenting books. This book is destined to be on the "must read" list for all adoptive parents.

> — Sarah H. Springer, MD, FAAP, chair, American Academy of Pediatrics Council on Foster Care, Adoption, and Kinship Care, and Kids Plus Pediatrics, Pittsburgh, PA

&

A gem of a book—adds to our knowledge of adoption of children at various ages and stages as well as circumstances from which children enter adoption. A must read for the new adoptive parent....

> — Victor Groza, PhD, LISW-S, Grace F. Brody Professor of Parent-Child Studies, Case Western Reserve University Mandel School

Caring for Your Adopted Child is a must read for anyone adopting.... [W]ith the expertise of a physician, the passion of a parent, and the encouragement of a coach, Dr Schulte demystifies the logistical, medical, social, and developmental concerns of adoption. With clear and practical advice, the authors provide a road map for anyone on this most wonderful of life's journeys.

> — Heather C. Forkey, MD, FAAP, director, Foster Children Evaluation Service and
> Child Protection Program, UMass Memorial Children's Medical Center

⚘

Caring for Your Adopted Child is an approachable and valuable resource for parents, pediatricians, and all professionals who care for adopted children. It could have been titled *What to Expect When You Are Adopting,* as it is an instructive and compassionate primer for parents who are preparing for adoption. Or it could have been titled *Understanding Your Adopted Child* because it provides critical insights for all caregivers on how to nurture adopted children into fulfilling their potentials.

> — Andrew Garner, MD, PhD, FAAP, coauthor of *Thinking Developmentally:*
> *Nurturing Wellness in Childhood to Promote Lifelong Health,* and clinical professor
> of pediatrics, Case Western Reserve University School of Medicine

⚘

Caring for Your Adopted Child is exactly what the extended family of adoption needs today. Packed with practical knowledge and delivered with a personal touch, Elaine and Robin have created a space for adoptive parents to be educated, empowered, and inspired as they love and care for their children. As a trans-racially adopted person, I applaud the American Academy of Pediatrics for making this resource available and signaling the importance of recognizing the nuances of caring for children and young people who have experienced separation from their families of origin.

> — April Dinwoodie, trans-racially adopted person, former chief executive,
> The Donaldson Adoption Institute

⚘

Dr Schulte and Ms Michaelson take the reader on a journey, beginning with pre-adoption consultations, to long-term post-adoption interventions, answering questions you don't even know you should ask! *Caring for Your Adopted Child* incorporates travel, medical, emotional, psychological, and educational advice and should be on every adoptive parent's bookshelf. It will be a reference guide for years to come.

> — Susan Orban, outreach and adoption specialist, Children's Home Society
> of Minnesota

Contributors

Authors
Elaine E. Schulte, MD, MPH, FAAP
Robin L. Michaelson

Reviewers
Amy Starin, PhD
Dipesh Navsaria, MD, MPH, MSLIS, FAAP
Heather Forkey, MD, FAAP
Tori Smith

American Academy of Pediatrics Staff Members
Lauren Barone
Mary A. Crane, PhD, LSW
Sunnah Kim
Karen Smith
Charlotte Zia

Dedication

To our families,
and all families who care for adopted children.

Contents

Foreword

Caring for Your Adopted Child is a book whose time has come. With close to 2 million adopted children who are living in the United States and millions of adult adoptees, I'm thrilled to see growing resources, such as this one, that recognize adopted people as having unique needs. Adoption is part of who that person is, not something that happened once.

Today, to the benefit of all involved, the understanding that adoption is a lifelong journey, rather than a onetime legal event, is now recognized as the standard of care. As an adoptee who grew up in the 1960s and 1970s, I know firsthand that this recognition wasn't always the case. While my parents were open with me and we discussed adoption freely at home, outside our home our family adoption was stigmatized and "swept under the rug." As a result, it wasn't talked about, taught about, or dealt with effectively.

As a child, I always asked a lot of questions, and I continued to ask questions as a registered nurse who was working in child psychiatry. Secrecy and denial were not promoted as healthy in any school of psychology. Why, then, were they the norm in our culture about adoption?

My personal and professional interests led me to found Adoption Network Cleveland: The Ohio Family Connection, a nonprofit organization now in its 30th year. I quickly learned through the hundreds of phone calls I received in the days following our first publicity just how many other adopted people also longed for a supportive community. This was an idea whose time had come. I have made adoption advocacy, education, and support my lifework.

So has Elaine Schulte, MD, MPH, FAAP, who I met when she was chair of General Pediatrics at the Cleveland Clinic and developing the Cleveland Clinic Children's adoption program. Dr Schulte, as an adoptive mom as well as a pediatrician, has been a strong and effective advocate for adoptive families. She has given parents a voice and resources that validate their experiences and safeguard their children. Her work spans decades through her clinics, her education of parents and other clinicians, and her service with the American Academy of Pediatrics and on the Board of Directors of Adoption Network Cleveland.

I'm thrilled Dr Schulte is sharing her personal and professional wisdom and expertise in this critical resource for adoptive parents. Dr Schulte, with her coauthor Robin L. Michaelson, walk through each step of the adoption journey with you: from getting ready to adopt, through attachment and emotional issues, through medical issues to be aware of, and through talking about adoption with your child. I believe the chapter on toxic stress and trauma-informed parenting is especially important because there is so much you, as parents, can do to understand and help your child.

Beyond being an important resource for parents, this book is also an important resource for adoption professionals, teachers, mental health professionals, medical providers, advocates, and anyone whose life has been touched by or who has a relationship with an adopted person. It's time we all built a sound understanding of what's best for children who are adopted and who may therefore have unique medical, developmental, behavioral, emotional, and psychosocial needs. This book will help all of us do our best for the adopted children in our lives.

Betsie Norris
Executive Director/Founder
Adoption Network Cleveland: The Ohio Family Connection

Please Note

The information and advice in this book apply equally to children and adolescents of both sexes, except where noted. To indicate this, we have chosen to alternate between masculine pronouns and feminine pronouns by chapter throughout the book.

The American Academy of Pediatrics recognizes the diversity of lifestyles and family arrangements. Please note that this advice applies equally to parents, single-parent families, partners, spouses, grandparents, and others involved in caring for children and adolescents.

The information contained in this book is intended to complement, not be a substitute for, the advice of your pediatrician. Before starting any medical treatment or program, you should consult with your pediatrician, who can discuss your child's individual needs and advise you about symptoms and treatment. If you have any questions about how the information in this book applies to your child, speak with your pediatrician.

This book has been developed by the American Academy of Pediatrics. Many of the contributors are expert authorities in the field of pediatrics. No commercial involvement of any kind has been solicited or accepted in the development of the content of this book.

Acknowledgments

We want to thank the American Academy of Pediatrics for all the work it does on behalf of supporting children and, in particular, for its recent focus on the needs of adopted children and children in foster care.

We are grateful to AAP Publishing, whose staff has supported this book from idea to publication. Special thanks to Mark Grimes for believing in and championing this book and to Kathryn Sparks for connecting us as writing partners and providing guidance through the process.

We are indebted to the AAP Council on Foster Care, Adoption, and Kinship Care. We want to acknowledge Elaine's colleagues on the council, particularly the members of the Executive Committee, who have shared their knowledge, energy, and passion for caring for adopted children for so many years. Thank you to Mary A. Crane, PhD, LSW, the program manager for the council, who has poured her heart into this work and kept all the council members on task, as they've authored many documents, including the AAP *Adoption Medicine* book, an extraordinary resource for physicians and adoption professionals.

From Elaine

I would like to begin by thanking all the adopted children and families who have shared their lives with me over the years. You trusted me to care for you, and I am very grateful to have gone on this journey together. Without you, we would have never been able to write this book.

I would also like to acknowledge the physicians who helped establish adoption medicine as a specialty. Thank you to all the pioneers, especially Drs Jane Aronson, Jerri Jenista, Dana Johnson, V. Faye Jones, Pat Mason, Laurie Miller, Todd Ochs, Lisa Albers Prock, Lisa Nalven, and Sarah Springer. You always remind me of the value of role models and mentors. Your clinical expertise, teaching, and advocacy work have provided constant inspiration.

Thank you to my AAP colleagues and to all my pediatric colleagues who have helped me provide medical care to adopted children and children in foster care. Thank you to the medical leaders in my academic health centers—Drs Martha Lepow, David Clark, Robert Wyllie, Jonathan Schaffer, Judy Aschner, and Daphne Hsu—all of whom sponsored and supported my adoption programs.

I am also grateful for the many education professionals—teachers, special education teachers, and administrators, particularly my friends at Lawrence School—who have dedicated their careers to children and who understand that great minds don't think alike. A special thank-you to the pediatric mental health providers who have taught me the significance of how important it is to help a child feel known and understood. And thank you to April Dinwoodie, Dr Heather Forkey, Betsie Norris, and Karen Rosenberg (for her wonderful interview!), for their contributions to this book.

Thank you to Robin, my coauthor, who listened to and then wrote about my experience using meaningful language in a parent-friendly voice. You made writing fun! And thank you to my wonderful friends, who were always able to provide support and advice when needed.

Last, thanks to Kim, Carly, and Lily—all of whom have provided daily inspiration and without whom, I never would have experienced the joy of being a parent and raising a family full of love.

From Robin

Thank you, Elaine, my wonderful writing partner and friend. Thank you to the families and colleagues who have worked with Elaine and generously shared their experiences and expertise with me. Thanks once more to Mark Grimes—I'm thrilled we could work together again on a book. I am grateful to my friends, especially Toni Burbank and Jillian Neubauer, who encouraged me to write this book because they know how much this topic means to me. I could not have done this without the love and support of my wonderful family. Thank you Mom and Patty. And thanks and love to Amelia and Willa—you made me a mom!—and to David, who shares this wonderful adventure with me.

Introduction

*C*ongratulations! You have made a commitment to become a parent! It doesn't matter whether you give birth or adopt (or do both). You have decided to welcome a child into your family. And every child deserves to be part of a loving and nurturing family.

Now, being part of a family isn't always easy, and it is possible that your child—whether he's biologically related to you or not—is going to give you a few extra gray hairs along the way. You are going to provide for your child no matter what. When issues arise, it's important to know that an adopted child has some extra puzzle pieces that make him unique. You won't know for sure how these puzzle pieces will influence your child's life, but it's crucial to remember that they exist and are part of who your child is.

I am an adoptive parent, as is my cowriter, Robin. We both love and care for our children no matter what, and we know you will too.

I'm also a pediatrician who specializes in adoption medicine. I have had the joy and privilege of working with hundreds of adopted children and their families for more than 20 years. When I first meet with an adoptive family, I always share some version of my thoughts based on my own experience. Of course, whether your child is adopted or not, all parents deal with the meals, the laundry, the playground, and school. You also experience your child's joy, laughter, tantrums, and tears. Becoming a parent is the start of a marvelous journey for both you and your child.

Yet, there is something unique to parenting an adopted child—be it an adoption from foster care or domestic or international adoption. We know—as adoptive parents and as an adoption medical specialist—there's more you need to know as an adoptive parent. For example, the American Academy of Pediatrics wonderful *Caring for Your Baby and Young Child: Birth to Age 5* shares what you need to know regarding the practical aspects of raising a child from the newborn period through kindergarten. However, you won't find detailed post-adoption information and advice in other parenting books, which is why we wrote this one.

In *Caring for Your Adopted Child,* we want to share with you the extra information adoptive families need to know that goes beyond traditional parenting advice. We discuss the medical, behavioral, and developmental challenges adopted children may experience from the first days following adoption throughout childhood and adolescence. Your child's pre-adoption history, including your child's family history, is an important part of who your child is. A child's pre-adoption life can affect his health and development and may present short- and long-term developmental and medical challenges. If you know what might happen and what to look for, you will be better able to help your child.

While this possibility might sound a little scary, we want to prepare you for the additional issues that you *may* experience as you parent your adopted child. We want to share with you what to watch for and when you should be concerned.

Children thrive in a loving and nurturing home. Even though your adopted child has an increased chance of having some medical and developmental issues, children are incredibly resilient. And your parenting can help make a difference. Children are most likely to overcome adversity when they have consistent, loving caregiving by an adult.

Adopted children may experience unique health, developmental, behavioral,

> "Genetic and prenatal and postnatal influences and an individual child's own resilience all contribute to differential outcomes in child development and overall well-being following adverse experiences."
> —*Lisa Nalven, MD, MA*

or emotional challenges. We review some immediate medical issues that need to be managed. Developmental delays, such as language delays, as well as gross and fine motor delays, are common, whether adopting domestically from foster care or internationally. We also discuss how parents can be attuned to certain emotional, attention, and learning challenges. Some adopted children struggle with difficult behavior from time to time. Your child may experience adoption-related grief and loss, at different ages, as he grows up. Age at adoption can affect psychological development. The older your child is, at the time of adoption, the more likely he is to have some struggles. Finally, as your child gets older, it's important to watch for mood disorders, increased levels of anxiety, and low self-esteem.

What You Do and Don't Know About Your Child's Health

Adoptive parents often have little to no information about their child's family medical history, the pregnancy of their child's birth mother, or their child's postnatal life circumstances. Sometimes the information is unreliable. Even when an adoption is domestic and open, a birth mother's prenatal history may be incomplete. A child's health can be affected by prenatal exposure to substances such as drugs and alcohol as well as maternal nutrition and stress. Often the circumstances of birth may be unknown. If a child has been in foster care or an institutional setting, he may have received poor-quality early caregiving or he experienced possible malnutrition, poor hygiene, limited stimulation, or physical or sexual abuse. Parents can work with their pediatrician to screen and monitor their child's health. Better caregiving immediately helps. Parents will need to have an ongoing sensitivity to what's known and what's not known.

In this book, we guide you through the various stages of adoptive family life. The first part of *Caring for Your Adopted Child* focuses on the immediate concerns you might have when your child joins your family. The second part of the book discusses what you should watch for along the way. We discuss what you might expect regarding possible growth, developmental, behavioral, and psychological challenges. The final part covers the always-present "as a family" themes for situations specific to adoptive families, such as talking openly about adoption and the importance of maintaining connections with the child's birth family.

The Changing Face of Adoption

When I first started seeing adopted patients more than 20 years ago, most adoptions were private domestic adoptions of newborns or adoptions from foster care. In the 1990s, after China and Eastern Europe opened their doors, the number of internationally adopted children began to increase dramatically. Dozens of children began arriving at doctors' offices, and most of us had little knowledge about how to care for them. I relied on my experience with taking care of children in foster care and reached out to a few colleagues around the country. We figured out how to screen for and manage the urgent medical issues, but we didn't know what the long-term trajectory would be like for these children. Over the past decade, we have become much more aware of how a child's early life experiences can affect him over time. As a general pediatrician specializing in adoption medicine, I've been incredibly fortunate to watch many adopted children grow up, and I have learned to always think about the impact that adoption has on their development.

Even if your pediatrician doesn't specialize in adoptions, she has probably cared for a number of adopted children, because many families create families through adoption. According to the 2010 US Census,[1] some 1.5 million adopted children live in the United States, comprising approximately 2% of the child population. Of that group, about 38% joined families through adoption from foster care, an equal percentage joined families through private domestic adoption, and 25% joined families through international adoption.[1,2]

Since 2010, I've noticed—and the numbers confirm—that the number of adoptions from domestic sources, including foster care, has been increasing, while international adoptions have declined. The most recent figures show that every year approximately 120,000 children are adopted.[1,2] The American Academy of Pediatrics estimates that 4 of 10 adopted children are part of transracial families.[3]

Beyond the numbers, I have seen many changes in the way families are created (and not just adopted families). More children are being placed long-term with relatives, what's known as "kinship" care. There are also more single-parent adoptions of children as well as same-sex couples who are adopting children together.

Another change that I've noticed is an increase in the number of adopted children with special health care needs. Many adopted children have complex medical, developmental, behavioral, educational, or psychological challenges. Research shows that 39% of adopted children were classified as having special health care needs, compared with 19% in the general population.[4] More than half of children adopted from foster care were considered to have special health care needs. And over the past several years, I've seen more and more children adopted from China with known special health care needs.

> "The preponderance of research suggests that even the majority of children with special needs adopted at older ages have positive outcomes with their adoptive families."
> —*Lisa Albers Prock, MD, MPH*

International Adoption

The number of international adoptions was at an all-time high of nearly 23,000 in 2004, but it has steadily declined for the past 12 years, according to 2016 State Department statistics.[5] There are many reasons for this change. Some countries are encouraging in-country adoption, such as China and Korea. Other countries have closed adoptions to the United States, while other countries have stopped international adoption because of questionable ethical practice.

Domestic Adoption

The number of domestic adoptions of newborns has remained mostly steady from 2007, according to the National Council for Adoption survey.[6] What has changed is that more adoptions are open—the family has open information and contact with the birth parents—rather than closed—the adoptive family has no or very limited information about the birth parents. More than one-third of children in nonrelative adoptions have had some contact with their birth parents.

Adoption From Foster Care

Since 2012, more children are entering the foster care system each year and are remaining in foster care, according to the Adoption and Foster Care Analysis Reporting System report.[7] However, the number of children adopted from foster care has increased from approximately 52,000 in 2012 to 57,000 in 2016.[8] Many of these children are older, have existing medical issues, and have experienced trauma. Some areas around the country have reported an increased demand for foster parents to care for babies born to mothers with opioid use.

Why Us

Both Robin and I are adoptive parents, and we both adopted daughters from China. We joined forces to write this book to share our practical and personal experiences, as well as my professional expertise as a pediatrician who has established and run 3 adoption medicine programs. Over the past 25 years, I have cared for hundreds of domestically adopted children and internationally adopted

No Two Families Are the Same

Adoptive families come in all shapes and sizes. Some families may be one-parent families, while others may be same-sex–couple families. Others may have a parent and a grandparent. Some of you will be first-time parents, while others will be adding to their families. Some of you may be related to the child you are adopting (kinship adoption) or have an open relationship with a birth mother or birth parents. Because no two families are the same, we realize that you may not be able to relate to everything we say, but we hope you will find value in what we've chosen to share. Wherever possible, we have included specific advice about children adopted domestically, internationally, or through foster care.

children, from nearly 20 countries, including China, Russia, Ukraine, South Korea, Guatemala, Haiti, Colombia, Ethiopia, Bulgaria, the Congo, Tanzania, India, Kazakhstan, Nepal, Morocco, Taiwan, and the Philippines. I have also provided care to hundreds of children in foster care.

Elaine's Story

In 1996, my spouse and I decided to create our family through adoption. In 1998, when I traveled to China to adopt our second daughter, I sat in a hotel lobby with other "expectant" parents and listened to their questions and worries. "How much formula should we feed her?" "How soon can we give her a bath?" "What if she has a fever?" As a pediatrician, I knew the answers and shared them. As I listened, I realized that while I had conducted hundreds of prenatal visits, I had never considered that prospective adopting parents could benefit from a similar type of "before you become a parent" visit.

During our own adoption process, as waiting parents, we had never heard of a pre-adoption visit with a pediatrician that was designed to help us get ready. No one suggested we talk with a medical professional to review our new daughters' medical records. I thought, *What a wonderful opportunity awaited me to help these adoptive parents prepare and then parent their adopted children.* Unlike a birth mother who delivers her baby in a hospital, an adoptive parent is often far away from home when she first meets her child. If adoptive parents have traveled to another state for a domestic adoption, they may have little or no immediate support from friends or family. If they are adopting internationally, they will be in another country, where they may not speak the language or understand certain cultural practices.

So, in 1997, at the urging of my spouse, when I went back to work after an adoption leave, I created an International Adoption Program in the Department of Pediatrics at Albany Medical College in New York. (I received wonderful advice from colleagues who are experts in adoption medicine and foster care and do what I do. Some of us help parents with pre-adoption consultations over the phone and through e-mail. Others will offer to meet you in person. (You can obtain a list of experts through the American Academy of Pediatrics Web site at www.aap.org/en-us/about-the-aap/Councils/Council-on-Foster-Care-Adoption-and-Kinship-Care/Pages/Leadership.aspx.) This comprehensive adoption program included a pre-adoption consultation for parents, travel support, post-adoption evaluation, and ongoing primary care. The pre-adoption consultation was designed to provide a thorough review of all medical records, photos, and videotapes. (Remember, in the late 1990s, there were no JPEG or WAV files!)

I also talked in-depth with parents about feeding, sleeping, behavioral expectations and challenges, and how best to transition a child from an orphanage or a foster care environment into a new family. I wanted families to understand that food and love could not "fix" everything that had gone "wrong" before adoption. Most important, I wanted families to have 24/7 access to someone who understood what they were going through before, during, and after adoption. Even though I wanted to make sure parents could understand the medical information, I wanted to share critical information and advice, so parents would understand what their child's world may have been like before the adoption, and how they could help their child make a smooth transition into their new family. I have performed hundreds of these consultations over the years, and I have been thrilled to share my knowledge and experience, both as a pediatrician and as a parent.

I also provided thorough post-adoption evaluations. I worked with my colleagues around the country to establish guidelines for appropriate medical tests. We talked about interpreting immunization records and about how best to know which vaccines were necessary to make sure newly adopted children were age appropriately immunized.

As a primary care pediatrician, I had the immense privilege of following many of these children in my office practice over many years. It took me a while to realize that while the early medical conditions were interesting, because one was never sure what would be found through the post-adoption evaluation, watching an adopted child grow up was fascinating! The rapid catch-up growth and development was exciting to see month after month. Sometimes within a year or two, I might start to worry about a developmental delay, or a new behavioral issue would crop up. Were these issues related to the adoption or not? How could we know? How could I help parents understand? This ongoing practice of caring for adopted children and their families was a work in progress.

In 2007, I moved back to my hometown of Cleveland to join Cleveland Clinic Children's. I founded the Clinic's adoption program, serving as the medical director. My practice grew quickly, and, as the demographics of adoption changed, I started seeing many more adopted children with special health care needs and seeing more children adopted from foster care. My need for pediatric subspecialists increased, as did the need for mental health services, as we all began to recognize and understand the implications of early childhood trauma.

After spending 10 years at the Cleveland Clinic, I moved to the Children's Hospital at Montefiore, in the Bronx, in 2017, and have established a new adoption program there as well.

Robin's Story

Robin is also an adoptive parent, who has edited many books in the parenting field. She has continued to edit and write while raising her 2 daughters. Robin and her husband adopted their older daughter (now a teenager) from China when she was 12 months of age.

Robin remembers...

Caring for Your Adopted Child includes what I wish I had known all in one resource. Because I live in the New York City area, I was able to consult with an international adoption medical specialist, who carefully guided me throughout the process. When we were in China, we called her from our hotel room, and she pulled over to the side of the road to answer our questions. I also brought my daughter for regular visits with her to complement my daughter's day-to-day pediatric visits. I relied on her, with her adoption expertise, to explain certain adoption-related behaviors and medical concerns. Now after more than a decade of parenting, I have discovered much I needed to know and be aware of, so I hope to share that wisdom with other adoptive parents. The more I knew, the better prepared I was to handle the challenges and concerns that cropped up. And I want all adoptive parents to have access to Elaine's adoption expertise to guide them on this

> ## *Robin remembers...(continued)*
>
> remarkable parenting journey. As one mom I interviewed told me, she wished everyone "could have an Elaine." She elaborated, "Parents need to find someone like her, someone who will help them take a deep breath, explain what is going on, and reassure them that it will be OK."

How This Book Proceeds

We start in Chapter 1 with advice on how to get ready before you meet your child. You may be traveling nationally, traveling internationally, or finalizing a foster care adoption.

In Chapter 2, we note your adjustment to being a family. All adoptive families experience a transition period, but what can you do to make the transition smoother? We also cover some of the immediate challenges with sleep, eating, bathing, and toileting, and we cover how to get through the rough spots.

Chapter 3 demystifies your child's first doctor's visit. Since prior medical information may be lacking or scarce, an adopted child's first medical examination will be more thorough than a typical doctor's visit. Even if you are not working with an adoption medical specialist, this chapter gives you what you need to know to make sure your child's first evaluation is as complete as possible. We walk you through all the additional tests adopted children require and also special concerns related to foster care.

Chapter 4 covers the follow-up visit, after you've settled in as a family. This is the time to evaluate the ongoing health and development of your child and how you're doing as a family.

Chapter 5 addresses specific health conditions because many adopted children have preexisting health conditions, ranging from prenatal exposure to drugs or alcohol to a cleft lip and palate.

Note to Our Readers

We decided to write in the first person, since Elaine is the physician in the house. We also alternate pronouns between *he* and *she* by chapter when we refer to children, for readability. Except where noted, information in this book applies equally to children of both sexes.

We have changed the names and identifying details of the parents and children we describe in the book to protect their privacy.

Throughout the book, we use "floating quotes," excerpts from the American Academy of Pediatrics reference *Adoption Medicine: Caring for Children and Families* unless otherwise specified. This marvelous manual, published in 2014, is a resource for medical and mental health professionals. We wanted to share with you adoption medicine research. Each floating quote lists the author(s) of the chapter it is from.

Please note that the information contained in this book is intended to complement, not be a substitute for, the advice of your child's pediatrician.

In Chapter 6, we discuss attachment. Parents are most often concerned about how their child is bonding with them. As children learn to trust their new environment, they sometimes experience a roller coaster of emotions, which can be quite upsetting for parents. How do parents handle these emotional outbursts while continuing to be nurturing? In this chapter, we explain attachment's ongoing process and its underlying patterns and offer strategies to aid a family in this process.

Chapter 7 focuses on your child's emotional health. It may be hard to accept that he may have experienced malnutrition, neglect, or even physical or sexual abuse. We also show how toxic stress and early childhood trauma can affect a child, including possible post-traumatic stress disorder. Despite adverse histories, children can be incredibly resilient, and we share with parents what they can do to help with recovery and healing.

Chapter 8 covers the learning and attention challenges many adopted children face. Language delays, learning differences, and attention challenges can be interrelated, and throughout your child's school experience, it's important to understand and be on the lookout for any difficulties. We also describe ADHD (attention-deficit/hyperactivity disorder) and sensory integration disorder.

Chapter 9 describes the all-important task of talking with your child openly and honestly about adoption. A child's understanding of what adoption means is different at different ages. As a parent, you will want to keep the adoption conversation open, flowing, and supportive. We share how to talk about adoption at different stages of your child's emotional development, and we encourage you to empathize with adoption-related losses and fantasies.

Your Journey Begins Now

Some of my greatest moments as a physician occur when I watch what happens as a child grows up. I've seen children who refuse to make eye contact become very engaging and funny children. I've seen a child who had barely any leg strength become a soccer star. And I've seen so many parents, who have given selflessly and tirelessly, take surprise and delight at what their child gives back—an endless supply of love and joy.

CHAPTER 1

Getting Ready to Bring Your Child Home

*Our adoption agency gave Andrew and me a list of
American Academy of Pediatrics pediatricians who
performed pre-adoption consultations. Before we
adopted, I called several to see how easy it was to
reach them and how quickly they returned my call.
I wanted to make sure I felt comfortable talking
with a doctor I'd never met before. A few weeks after
I selected our doctor, we got a call from the agency—
we were matched! The agency wanted us to review
the baby's medical information and make our decision
within a day. I was glad I had a doctor to reach out to.
She called us back within a few hours, and she helped
us make an informed decision.*

> — *Gwen, mother of Hannah, a domestically
> adopted child*

*A*s a physician, I've been trained to always be ready for anything, and this trait is also a natural part of my personality. I like to prepare and plan so I know what's going to happen before it does. Of course, life doesn't always work like this, but I still believe that a certain degree of preparation for most situations can help relieve our anxieties. At least it helps relieve mine!

The Value of a Pre-adoption Consultation

While a pre-adoption consultation is not a required part of the adoption process, most adoption agencies recommend that prospective parents talk with a pediatrician who has expertise in adoption. The American Academy of Pediatrics posts a list of adoption medical specialists on its Web site (www.healthychildren. org/English/tips-tools/find-pediatrician/Pages/Pediatrician-Referral-Service.aspx). These pediatricians will review any medical records, photos, and video files of your child, and they will answer any questions you have. Please keep in mind, however, that no pediatrician will tell you whether a child is "right for you" or whether you should "accept the referral." Pediatricians who perform pre-adoption consultations want to help you make an informed decision. And they might talk about some aspects of adoption that are difficult to hear—for example, the risks of early childhood trauma and how much a birth mother's prenatal history may affect a child's life. Again, these physicians are sharing their professional opinions based on their own experiences. You don't have to agree with what the physician says, but do take note. Feel free to ask lots and lots of questions and to ask for further clarification if you don't understand an answer.

Any pediatrician who assists families during the pre-adoption period might offer a range of different services and will understand the importance of being available quickly. Some offer a onetime medical record review. Others will maintain ongoing contact during the pre-adoption period and will continue to answer your questions. If you are traveling, some will help you prepare as you get ready, and some will also provide the option for you to contact them during your trip. You will want to ask your physician about response time and to clarify with your physician expectations about what services are included and for what length of time. Most, but not all, pediatricians charge a fee for their adoption consultations. Some pediatricians who perform pre-adoption consultations also perform the recommended comprehensive post-adoption evaluation (see Chapter 3). And some of these physicians will provide ongoing primary care for your child.

Robin remembers…

I remember how hard it was to go through the adoption process and to feel different from pregnant friends. I knew about all the forms, the fingerprinting, the home study, the clearances, and the piles of required paperwork. I also knew that the adoption process is very much a "hurry up and wait" kind of experience. Some days, the waiting would seem intolerable. We would call our adoption agency for an update only to learn that things were "pushed back." I knew how hard it was waiting for the referral to come. I remember waiting for the call and then the e-mail with our daughter's photo and paperwork. My husband and I opened the photo file at the same time. We couldn't wait to see her face! Then we looked at the medical paperwork, which was in Chinese; our agency also provided a translation. Because we had established a relationship with an adoption medical specialist, I knew I could forward the medical records immediately, and our doctor would be able to review and understand the documents. We were going to say yes, but we had a few questions. Our doctor answered our questions and understood our impatience and excitement.

Even if you have adopted before or you are an experienced parent, I recommend you establish a relationship with a pediatrician who is familiar with adoption.

What Parents Ask Me About Adoption

I always tell all parents—whether they've adopted or not—that there are no "stupid" questions. If you don't know something and you want an answer, just ask. You are doing your job as a parent. Some parents have no idea what to ask during these pre-adoption consultations, and that's OK. Even a question such as "How much should I feed her the first day?" is a great question. Here are my answers to pre-adoption questions that I'm often asked.

She looks so healthy in the picture. Is she going to be OK?

"Is my child going to be OK?" is the crucial question. I wish I could always tell parents that their child is going to be healthy. The reality is that no one can offer that type of reassurance. For all the reasons you'll read about later in this book, it is impossible to guarantee—or know—that any child is going to be healthy, even if the child's medical records indicate that that might be the case. When a child develops a medical condition or a mental health concern, pediatricians often don't know the reason. Adopted children are at greater risk of certain conditions that can affect a child's overall health, which we discuss in later chapters. Our job, as pediatricians, is to provide the support and education to ensure that every child receives appropriate medical care.

Do you recommend we meet our child's birth mother?

If you have an opportunity to have an open adoption, I would recommend you do. An open adoption establishes a foundation of honesty about everyone's life circumstances. It reduces the association of shame and guilt that used to be so much a part of what adoption meant. These days, most people are highly supportive of open adoptions. Your child will want—and need—to know about her birth family, and her birth family may want to know about her as well. While circumstances at some future point might make regular contact difficult, meeting your child's birth mother (and father) and finding out as much as you can now will be very helpful in the long run.

I'm adopting from foster care. Can I talk with you about the preplacement visits?

Yes, you can ask questions about anything that comes up during preplacement visits. Your physician may also have some questions for you about what you have observed. Preplacement visits are a wonderful way to help you and your child establish some continuity and will help as she transitions from a foster home to your home.

What should I bring on the trip?

Nowadays, it often doesn't matter whether you are traveling to the next state or around the world to adopt. You can usually get what you need right where you are. But since I believe in my "be prepared" motto, here are several items that I recommend you always have handy.

Food

Food is critical! Depending on how old your child is, you may have to prepare baby formula, so always have some extra with you. You do not need to use boiled water, but you do need to use bottled water if you are out of the country. You will also want to have some type of nonperishable healthy snacks, if your child is older than 9 to 12 months. A hungry child is an unhappy child.

Medical supplies

You won't need a lot of medical supplies, but I suggest bringing some type of fever-reducing medication and medication to treat an allergic reaction. Your pediatrician can give you an estimation of how much medication to give, based on your child's weight. (Note that if your child is a newborn and has a fever, you will need to take your child to an emergency department for evaluation.) If your child is vomiting or has diarrhea, you may need to use a rehydrating solution, so bring some along. You can mix the packets of rehydrating solution with bottled water. You will also want to have some type of over-the-counter antibacterial ointment to treat minor skin infections. And remember to bring any medications you take.

I generally recommend that you do not need to bring antibiotics. If your child becomes sick enough to require antibiotics, I would recommend that you take her to a local physician or hospital. You can also reach out to your pediatrician for advice. Robin remembers calling her adoption medical specialist, who, several time zones away, pulled over to the side of the road to take her call.

Clothing

Sometimes it's hard to know exactly how big your child will be, so I suggest taking a few sets of clothes in different sizes. If you are a new parent, bring clothing that is super simple to put on and take off. Dressing a toddler can sometimes feel like a wrestling match! Also, pay attention to the type of clothing your child is wearing when you meet her. Is she in layers or dressed lightly? Are her clothes tight or loose fitting? You will want to keep her dressed as much the same as possible to help the transition.

Diapers

Parents often wonder whether they should bring diapers for an older child. Even if your child's medical records state that your child is toilet-trained, I would still pack some diapers or training pants (eg, Pull-Ups). Many children are accustomed to sitting on a potty every 2 hours, so the assumption is often made that they are toilet-trained. When the routine changes during the transition, your child may start to have accidents. What might be going on? Perhaps your child has never really been toilet-trained, so she hasn't developed the "bladder talking to brain" mechanism. Or, she doesn't know yet how to signal or communicate to you that she needs to use the bathroom. In addition, many children regress and resort to pre-potty behavior when their lives get turned upside down. If your child starts having accidents, please support her. She's confused, not misbehaving. Put a diaper or Pull-Up on her. You will all be happier, and you can work on toileting skills when you are home.

Toys

Parents almost always ask me how many and what type of toys they should bring. If you are adopting a newborn, toys aren't really necessary. Your newborn will do what all newborns do—namely, eat, sleep, and poop! You will stimulate her by making great eye contact, talking, singing, and swaddling. If you are adopting an older child, she may or may not have had exposure to toys, and it is highly unlikely that she will have had an overwhelming amount of play items. So, if you pack toys my advice is (1) the simpler, the better and (2) the fewer, the better. Try to find 2 or 3 toys that stimulate different types of senses—for example, visual, auditory, and touch. Bring a stuffed animal or blanket. I'm also a fan of age-appropriate books, especially board books. But don't be too surprised if your child has never seen a book. Try to read to her, but know she may reject that idea since it's a new activity. Also, don't be alarmed if your child has no clue how to play with her toys or stuffed animal. You can teach her and model caregiving and cuddling behaviors.

How will my new son/daughter react to me?

"How will my new son/daughter react to me?" is another difficult question to answer. Even if I could predict your child's initial response, most likely her response to you will change over time. Remember that most children, even older children, can't really process what's happening. Some children are very excited initially and may jump into your lap and put their hands in your face, pull your earrings, or tug at your beard. Others may refuse to make eye contact and may shy away from you. Some children won't stop crying. Babies may be fairly easy to console, but not always, and without language, it can be really challenging to understand why any child is upset.

No matter how your child reacts, my advice is to stay calm and take the cues from your child. Don't insert yourself too quickly into a situation. Try to think about what it's like to be your child and what might be going on for her. Use a soft, reassuring voice and get on the same level as your child, which might mean sitting on the floor. Sometimes, being there for your child is all she needs.

Depending on your child's age and developmental level, try to find something that might interest her. But don't offer a lot of toys or options quickly. Doing so might further disorient her. Instead, give her time to relax. She will respond eventually, but doing so may take a few minutes, a few hours, or even a few days. I promise that you will connect with your child. I just can't promise when.

How will I feel?

All I can tell you is that the experience of adoption will feel a bit surreal. Robin and I both felt this way—all the preparation and the waiting and the expectations and the feelings converged at once. You may find yourself filled with joy *and* terrified. You may witness your child's birth, which can be a very frightening experience if you've never seen a child being born, or it may seem like the most beautiful thing in the world. You may feel as if you've made a mistake, you have no business being a parent, and you don't know what you're doing. All these reactions are within the expected range of emotions. When you feel overwhelmed, notice the feeling and acknowledge it. If you can share it with someone, that will help too.

What to Do Before Your Child Comes Home

Check your own health

It's a good idea to see your own physician to make sure you are in good health! If you are traveling internationally, check in with your physician or go to a travel clinic, as you may need immunizations to protect you from diseases endemic to the country you're traveling to.

If it's flu season, get a flu vaccine, regardless of whether you're traveling. Even if you don't typically get a flu vaccine, you are now a parent, and your child is more susceptible to the flu than you are. If your child gets sick, there's a good chance that you are going to get sick as well. If you are sick, you can't take good care of your child.

Get into shape

Before your child comes home may be the last time you really get to focus on your physical well-being. Being a parent is exhausting, both physically and emotionally. If you are not in great shape and are not used to moving, holding, or carrying children, your body will ache right away. If you are adopting a young child or an infant, I suggest purchasing a baby carrier of some sort and putting a 15-lb bag of cat litter in it and wearing it in your home. If you've been meaning to learn yoga or start swimming, do it! You will feel better and can try to continue these practices after your child arrives. What an excellent way to role model a healthy lifestyle for your child.

Set up your child's room

Since most parents have already thought of how they want to set up their child's room, I like to remind parents to think about the environment that their child has been sleeping and living in, and I like to suggest that they try to duplicate this environment as best they can. Doing so does not mean filling a child's room with dozens of toys and games or having brightly colored walls, bedding, and furniture. Keep your setup simple. If your child lived in a foster home with 3 other children and shared bunk beds in a small bedroom, she may be extremely unhappy alone in a queen-sized bed. If your child slept in an orphanage, it was probably pretty noisy with the sounds of crying children. Being in a quiet, dark room may be very scary. You might have to make some changes after you come home. See how your child reacts to her room, and make any necessary adjustments. Being flexible is an essential parenting skill.

Knock a few items off your bucket list

Before your child comes home may be the last time you have some adult freedom for a while. Travel to that place you always wanted to visit. Check in with your former roommate from college. Read that novel that's been waiting for you. Go skydiving. Take the cooking class. Be kind to yourself.

Meeting Your Child for the First Time

The van pulled up to the hotel, and the door opened. There she was! Sara looked so much smaller than we'd imagined. Her caregiver brought her inside. The minute she set her down, Sara started to cry—and she cried the rest of the day. We couldn't do anything to console her. She hated being held. She refused to eat or nap. She didn't seem interested in any of the toys we brought along. We were distraught. This was not how we thought meeting her would go.

— Dave and Janet, meeting their 10-month-old daughter for the first time

What to expect the day of

The day has arrived. Maybe you're going to be in the delivery room, or maybe you're going to be halfway around the world. Maybe it's the day your foster child officially becomes your adopted child. Maybe you've been waiting for years for this day to come, or maybe it's happened much faster than you anticipated. Whatever the circumstances, you are adding a new member to your family. Congratulations! You will remember this day forever, and you will tell your son or daughter this story over and over.

I know that most parents feel pretty nervous. They don't sleep well the night before. They misplace their car keys, they don't know when they last ate, or they forget to bring something with them that they need. I let them know that these reactions are typical and expected. Who would sleep well the night before their family composition changes forever? Neither Robin, nor I, nor our spouses, did.

While adoption marks a beginning of something, adoption also denotes an ending of something else. This "something else" may be hard to think about, but it's important that you do. While your adopted child has a new family, she has "lost" her birth family. (Even if you have an open-adoption arrangement, your child will still experience a loss.) While the adoption has most likely been a consensual decision, it was probably a very difficult one. You may never fully know the angst your child's birth parent (or parents) experienced around the adoption placement. This lack of knowledge may haunt you, and it may haunt your child at various times. With understanding, openness, and love, you can look forward to integrating any feelings of loss, and acceptance, into your lives together.

On this day, please acknowledge and honor your child's birth parent in a meaningful way. I believe there is value in intentionally appreciating special events like this. Take a moment to yourself.

Breathe. Step outside and look at the sky. Find a way to savor this memory, and tuck it into your heart. You can share this memory with your child as part of the story of this special day. Adoption is bittersweet for sure.

A few tips in advance

On a more practical note, here are a few suggestions that might help your first few days with your child go better.

Always take cues from your child

For most parents, the first few days can be pretty scary. Think of parenting like being a detective, especially with a child who can't tell you what she needs or wants. Please take time to observe your child, because it's likely that you don't know anything about her (and the likewise is true as well!). What does she like? What makes her laugh? What is she afraid of? What does she want more of? Try to keep things as simple as possible. Don't feel as if you need to entertain your child by constantly stimulating her. You don't need to leave your hotel and find fun things for her to do. Too much stimulation can be overwhelming. She will eventually let you know—and you will figure out—what keeps her content.

Hold off on that strong urge to clean or bathe your child and to put new clothes on her

You may wonder why I don't suggest changing your child immediately into new clothes. I don't because she will be most comfortable in the clothes she's in. She's used to the feel and smell. And this familiarity may be the only reassuring part of her identity that she can hold on to as this transition happens. If possible, try to keep her in the same clothes for the day and to bathe her later, as she becomes more comfortable with you.

Figure out feeding

You may want to feed your baby or toddler, and she may not want nothing of it. Or, your child may have no idea how to feed herself, and you have to help her. Don't worry if she doesn't want to try new foods or drink from a new cup. Or, your baby might reject a bottle if the baby formula tastes different or if the bottle has a different nipple. She will learn.

You may find that your child may be really hungry, and you can't get food in fast enough. Don't worry. You both will figure out a rhythm of feeding that works for everyone. Since you might not be entirely sure of her feeding history, introduce new foods slowly. Make sure your child can handle the volume and texture of each bite. It's unlikely that she will have an allergic reaction to new foods, but go slowly just in case.

Call your "A-Team" when you need help

Know whom to contact in case of an emergency. If you are traveling out of town, take the names and numbers of your physicians, your child's soon-to-be physician, and your adoption agency. Share your itinerary with family and close friends. Robin and I remember traveling to China and having to make long-distance calls and barely having e-mail access. Today, communication is instant and easier!

Don't hesitate to call your "A-Team" if you need help or feel as if you could use some emotional support. You will be of no use to your family if you aren't at your best and feeling physically well. Rest, eat, and ask others for help. Continue to take care of yourself.

Keep a journal or list of questions for your child's first pediatric visit

Writing a list of questions may sound a little silly, but you are going to be tired and overwhelmed at your child's first pediatric visit. It's easy to forget everything you want to ask.

Note your child's routine

Your pediatrician will ask you questions too. She will want to know how every day is going. When are mealtimes? When does your child sleep? What happens during play? Try to get into a routine every day, so both you and your child know what to expect. If things don't go smoothly one day, try something different by varying the routine the next day. If you start to panic because you can't get into a routine, don't wait for the pediatric visit; instead, call your pediatrician.

Ask questions

Meeting your child for the first time may be the only time you get to talk with your child's birth mother or meet your child's foster parents or orphanage caregivers. You want to find out everything you possibly can about your child. I realize you may not be able to ask questions, or there may be a language barrier. Even if that's the case, please take photos, make observations, and record conversations. This step is important for you, but it will be essential for your child as she gets older and wants a sense of who she was before the adoption and what happened that day. These observations can be included in your child's life book (see Chapter 9).

If you have to travel with your child, you will survive

Taking young children through airports and on planes tends to be an unenjoyable experience. I always tell parents that if it was socially acceptable, we would all scream while flying! I also tell parents to *not* give a child any sort of sedating medication. It won't work. In fact, it may have the opposite effect. Children don't like the feeling of losing control and will sometimes respond with an increased level of agitation. Always pack extra food and clothing in your carry-on bag and have some small toys or age-appropriate games handy. If possible, have an extra adult along with you to help.

Take care of yourself while you are out of town

You may not be used to napping, but the experience of being out of town will be emotionally and physically exhausting. Nap when your child naps. Try to go to bed early. If you're dealing with jet lag, you will need the extra sleep anyway. Make sure to keep yourself well hydrated, and eat small, frequent, well-balanced meals.

Don't worry if you don't feel an immediate connection

It's OK if you don't feel an immediate connection with your child. You may feel a little let down or even sad or depressed during your trip or after you return home. Maybe your child isn't who you thought she'd be. Maybe she's not bonding the way you'd like her to. Maybe your mind is numb because all you're doing is household chores. These feelings are disconcerting and tough to have, but please know that they are fairly typical. Also, know that you can and should ask for help if any sadness or empty feelings start to overwhelm you. (See Chapter 4.)

Welcoming a Child to Your Family

The pre-adoption process may feel like a challenging time, but I hope this advice helps you feel more prepared. Even experienced parents, who are adopting again, worry about what the experience will be like. This is a major life transition for all of you. But always remember and fall back on your intention—you are welcoming a child into your family! How wonderful! It's a new beginning for everyone.

CHAPTER 2

A New Everything! Welcoming Your Child Home

Lena was lying flat on her back, asleep in her new bed. Kevin and Amy had waited so long for this day. They stood over their daughter, watching her breathe. They couldn't believe they were finally parents, after all the paperwork, training, and appointments that led up to the adoption, followed by the waiting. Now—all of a sudden—Lena was home. Overwhelmed by emotion, they wondered: What was she going to be like? Was she going to love them? Would things ever be the same? Were their hopes and dreams for their family going to come true?

— Kevin and Amy, parents of 4-year-old Lena

*C*ongratulations! Your child is home! You are a family!

For any adoptive family, change comes quickly. You may have been preparing for your new addition for many months, or you may have recently submitted all the paperwork and gotten a call sooner than expected. You may have traveled across the state or across the country to be in the hospital when your baby was born. You may have traveled internationally to bring your child home. Or, you may have finally received word that your foster child is now officially an adopted member of your family.

However your family came together, this stunning moment changes your life from before children to after children, from having children you know to adding one more to your family. Nothing can prepare you for the full-on press of being a parent. You have laundry to wash, meals and snacks to prepare, games to play, and appointments to attend. The day-to-day activity with a child of any age is both exhausting and rewarding.

When Robin adopted her daughter, she consulted the American Academy of Pediatrics parenting books for practical advice, such as how to take her daughter's temperature. But she also had questions that went beyond the books. *How was her daughter transitioning? How would she get used to everything being new? How well would she sleep and eat?*

We both vividly recall the moment our children made us moms. We remember how much love we felt, but we also recall how scared and stunned we were. And we understood that our children shared these feelings too.

A New Family

What's key is to remember that the transition into a new family is a transition for *everyone*. Both you and your child are experiencing an abrupt adjustment. Everyone is learning how to be a family

Your child may be grieving in his own way, which depends on his adoption story and his ability to connect with his grief. Not all children experience immediate grief, but many do. If your child has strong feelings around attachment to his caregivers, it is likely that he has learned to trust others and misses those who took care of him. He may be well aware of his sadness, or he may not be in touch with these feelings for years. Sometimes, children "shut down" completely as if they are in some other place. It's hard to know if they are experiencing grief or shock or even post-traumatic stress disorder. (See Chapter 7 for more on post-traumatic stress disorder.)

He may also be reacting from a place of stress or anxiety. Change is difficult, even terrifying, for a child. Stress induces the "fight or flight or freeze" response. Your child may be alert and hypervigilant, or he may be shut down or passive. Regardless, it's easy for him to feel overstimulated. He may be experiencing anxiety above and beyond what a child at the same age would be. He needs to learn to depend on you.

A younger child may find this transition to be hard to understand or process, while an older child—even though this transition may have been explained to him—has built up defenses and learned other ways of reacting to stress and anxiety. Older children may be more anxious. They are trying their best to follow rules they may not understand yet. If they can use their words, they may tell you that it's scary to go to sleep or that they're afraid of dogs. Younger children can't express themselves as easily, so they may have more unpredictable behaviors, such as tantrums.

While these behaviors may be hard to tolerate, please try to be patient and understanding, which we know is easier said than done. You will need to wait it out, as these behaviors could subside in a few days or a few months. Or, you may think that things are going along just fine, and then wham! You will see a behavior that catches you off guard.

Your child needs your comfort and support. Express empathy and acknowledge his feelings. This "new home" may feel all wrong to your child. It's not the way he was treated before. Even though you may be providing a healthier environment, it's still different. He's not rejecting you; rather, he may not be used to this new, safe, trusting, nurturing household.

Time to Be Together

I encourage my adoptive families to nest when they get home. What does *nesting* mean? It means spending time together as a family unit and limiting visitors in the home and experiences outside the home. It means that only you and any other primary caregiver can take care of your child—feeding him, bathing him, changing his clothes, diapering or toileting him, and putting him to sleep. It means creating a comfortable, safe, and nurturing environment for your child.

The Primary Caregiver

We use the term *primary caregiver* as we know that families come in different configurations. Your child's primary caregiver may be you, a couple, a parent and grandparent, or however your family chooses to care for your child.

When can my family and friends meet him?

Naturally, you are excited to introduce your child to your relatives and friends, and I'm not saying that's a bad idea. But it is a good idea to limit visits, with a few visitors at a time and for 20 minutes to a half hour. Acknowledge that you know they want to meet your child and help you, so ask for their help so you can focus full-time on your child. Ask them to run errands, go grocery shopping, or bring a meal. If you have other children, ask them to take those children out for a playdate. And if your extended family doesn't understand why they can't come over for extended periods of time, tell them that you are following the pediatrician's rules!

When is it OK to take him places?

I don't mean to suggest that you should stay only in your house with your child. It's fine to go outside or take a walk in your neighborhood. Local parks are fine too, if the other children playing there don't overwhelm your child. You might also want to take him on car rides around town. However, I wouldn't take your child to the mall, to work, or to your place of worship immediately. Please wait if you can, because these locations are very stimulating. Even though your child might seem to enjoy bright lights and meeting lots of people, he can be easily overwhelmed. There will be plenty of time for these excursions once he has adjusted.

How long is long enough?

"How long is long enough?" is a tough question to answer. Take your cues from your child. When he begins to explore his world, on his own, but turns to you for help and comfort, he's probably attaching well. He is learning whom he can trust. Take purposeful, short trips into your community and see how he does. You may have the luxury of waiting until he's ready, or, like many parents, you may need to return to work.

If you work, look into taking advantage of any parental leave your employer might offer. Sometimes, parents alternate time home if they can. It's helpful for your child to have consistent care from familiar caregivers as he adjusts to his new home and before he goes into child care or starts school. The adoption process may have used up much of your leave time. Please do the best you can! If one parent can be home full-time at first, that arrangement often works well for the transition. But I also know that doing so isn't practical for every family.

Establishing Routines

I always encourage families to establish routines. Even babies need to learn to trust their caregivers. They are helpless and depend on us. Your child needs to learn to trust you too. The consistency and familiarity of a routine helps your child become comfortable with the rhythms of your home, and this routine helps you, too, as you adjust to this new normal! Remember that you are doing things differently from what your child was used to. He might get upset when you lay him down to change a diaper, as that might remind him of being left in his crib or being restrained for a medical procedure. Being put to bed, alone, in a quiet room may be quite different from his sleeping situation before. If this routine seems challenging, spend some time in his bedroom during the day. Play quiet games there. Read to him in a comfortable chair. Make his bedroom a safe space. Help him learn how to comfort himself, in his room, before bedtime occurs. Let him select his favorite book. Keep special pictures of your new family or his birth family, if known, next to the bed, so he can refer to them if he wants comfort at night.

Making Your Home Your Child's Home

For an adopted child, who may have memory of his former living situation, it's important to help him make his new home feel like his. If he can tell you what he likes, offer choices for setting up his bedroom. "Would you like a blue pillow or a red one?" "Would you like to put your toys in a basket or on a shelf?" "Where should we put your lamp?"

Your child needs calmness and reassurance. As I mentioned earlier, it's easy for your child to feel overstimulated. Try to keep the household as quiet as possible. Of course, he will want to be noisy and play, so try to keep play from getting out of control or overwhelming. He has to learn to feel safe. You will meet his needs for love, food, and safety, but he may not "know" that yet. His world may still feel uncertain.

Sleep

John cried when we put him in the crib. We had to bring John into bed with us to get him to go to sleep. — Maddie

Lola cried herself to sleep, and then she cried out, during the night—I think she was having nightmares. — Nazar

Our daughter slept through the first night—we were the ones who kept waking to check on her. — Mariel

I get many questions from parents who are concerned about their child's sleep. I've heard it all—from the great sleepers from the get-go to the many children who struggle to fall and stay asleep. Sleep problems are common as children adapt to new sleep environments. Parents want to know the "magic" solution, but no one answer fits all children. However, I have tailored my advice for children who are adopted, because if an adopted child is struggling with sleep, his needs are different.

Struggles with sleep

Remember that your child does know how to fall asleep, because he fell asleep by himself in the orphanage or his prior foster home (or homes). This fact doesn't mean that falling asleep was a pleasant experience. You have the opportunity, in his new environment, to "wind the clock back" and teach him what to do if he is struggling to fall and stay asleep.

If you've adopted internationally, all of you will first need to recover from the jet lag and the exhaustion, both emotional and physical, from your trip. Resetting everyone's biological clock can take a few days to a few weeks, depending on how many time zones away you were. Children generally recover faster than adults do. Try staying awake as much as possible during the day, and expose yourself to as much natural light as possible. Start eating meals at regular or typical times. (Yes, at first, you will be hungry at 2:00 am. It's OK to have a snack then for the first few nights!)

If you've adopted from foster care, and your child is new to your home, help your child familiarize himself with his room. Spend time playing in the room during the day. Give your child some choices about what he might want in his room that might be comforting at night—for example, a night-light, a special stuffed animal, or a picture of something familiar.

Regardless of the type of adoption, your child may be chronically exhausted because of the nature of his care before meeting you. He may sleep way longer than you'd ever think. He may start taking naps, even if he'd outgrown them a year ago. If he's fighting to take a nap, because he's scared or doesn't want to separate from you, teach him about rest time. You may need to stay with him to help him settle. If he's so anxious that he can't settle, and he seems exhausted, take him for a car ride and hope he falls asleep. This effort may help jump-start a healthy sleep routine. For ongoing nighttime troubles with falling asleep, you may want to consider giving melatonin for a brief period to get him into a healthy sleep routine. Talk with your pediatrician about the right dosage for your child and how best to implement it.

Establishing a sleep routine

It's a good idea to establish a sleep routine, no matter your child's age. Here are some suggestions.

- Read books together, with him on your lap or next to you.
- Rock him in your arms, but put him into bed drowsy but still awake.
- Make him comfortable in his room/bed, turning down the lights and singing softly.
- Sit with him and hold his hand as he falls asleep.
- Stay in his room until he is comfortable.

If he wakes up in the night,

- Go into his room to reassure him. Rub his back, but don't pick him up.
- Try not to disturb him too much, so he stays drowsy.
- Don't turn on the lights.
- Make sure he has a "lovie" (blanket or stuffed animal) for comfort. (You may need to show him how to use it to soothe himself. He can use the lovie during the day too.)

I suggest parents *not* do the following things because these will create sleep problems, not solve them:

- Do not let him fall asleep in your arms. He will learn that this is the way he should fall sleep. While it may feel comforting for both of you, in the long run, he needs to learn to fall asleep on his own.
- Do not let him fall asleep drinking a bottle. This habit may harm his developing teeth.
- Do not keep a bottle in the crib. He will think that he's supposed to eat where he sleeps.

Common sleep questions

Q: Should I let my child sleep in my bed?

A: Never if he's younger than 12 months, because of the increased risk of sudden infant death syndrome. Other than that, whether you let your child sleep in your bed with you is up to you. I'm not in your home with you at 2:00 am when your entire household is awake and listening to a distressed child cry. However, if you allow him into your bed, that's where he will want to sleep. Expect that any behaviors you endorse early on will be the behaviors that linger—and you may have to break those habits later.

Why It's Lovely to Have a "Lovie"

My tween still sleeps with the doll we gave
her when we met her in China. — *Faith*

It's lovely to give your child a doll, a blanket, or another transitional object that he can use to comfort himself. He may also rub or tug at his ears, as a baby might do. Some children will rock themselves on the floor, or bang their heads, or pull their hair. These types of self-soothing behaviors will typically diminish in frequency over time.

To make your child's room more comfortable, you may want to plug in a night-light or use a white-noise machine. A quiet, dark bedroom may be very different from what your child is used to.

Q: Should I let him "cry it out"?

A: A newly adopted child should *never* "cry it out," no matter his age. Please go into your child's room to reassure him you are there. Over time, you can wait longer before going into his room as he learns to soothe himself. But he needs to know that you are there for him.

Q: Should I put up a gate so he can't wander out of his room to find me?

A: No. Fortunately, an older child who has slept in a bed is generally very compliant and doesn't tend to wander initially. This tendency can change, as he becomes more accustomed to his new environment, and he might want to seek you out for comfort. You don't want your child to feel trapped at night.

Q: How long will my child need to nap?

A: Napping depends on your child's age. Most children stop napping by age 5 years. However, if your child is having trouble falling asleep at night and is still napping, you might consider shortening daytime naps to increase nighttime sleep.

Feeding

Parents often tell me: "My son is eating anything *and* everything in sight—from eating peas, to eating crackers, to drinking gallons of milk. He clears his plate and asks for more. Should I give him more? Is it OK to let my child eat as much as he wants?"

My initial answer is yes, if the choices are healthy and meals occur at typical times. Your child will not develop obesity in the first months home. Early on, eating an excessive amount of food is very common. Your child may be transitioning from a situation in which he didn't know where his next meal was coming from or in which eating wasn't a social or pleasant experience. His body may not know what it truly feels like to be hungry or to be full. While he figures this behavior out, he may eat more than he truly needs, although many children need to eat more because they've been undernourished. I have found that most children will learn to self-regulate over time. They learn when they are hungry, and they notice when they are full.

If your child is younger than 12 months, you can introduce new foods slowly, varying tastes and textures. For older children, you may want to mix familiar foods with new ones and let your child choose healthy options. Over the years, most children I've cared for learn to become excellent and adventurous eaters.

Parents can help by modeling good eating habits, which include 4 to 5 servings of fruits and vegetables, healthy grains, a protein serving at every meal, and 3 to 4 servings of dairy per day. Some children won't get to this point for a while, but they watch what their parents (and siblings—if present) do. So, please model healthy eating behaviors. Serve meals in your kitchen or dining room. Don't let your child wander about the house with food. If your child needs a snack, provide healthy choices.

If your child is malnourished or underweight

If your child is malnourished or underweight, it's best for him to eat nutrient-dense foods. For drinks, *nutrient-dense* means no water or juice. Instead, offer yogurt smoothies or cow's milk when your child is thirsty. You want to maximize calories in the beginning. You can add water to his diet later, depending on his age and nutritional status; talk with your pediatrician.

If obesity is a concern

If your child is adopted from foster care, he has an increased risk of developing overweight or obesity. For this reason, it's wise to offer water as a beverage at snack time. Dairy servings can be offered at mealtimes and, once a child has turned 2 years of age, should be reduced fat.

I suggest that parents give children some autonomy around food choices without being too restrictive. Of course, this autonomy can be tough at times, as most children will push limits, saying they are "still hungry" or they want "more dessert." It is also quite possible that a newly adopted child doesn't really know what hungry versus full feels like. He will figure this feeling out over time, and your role, as his parent, is to help him. Talk about what foods he likes and doesn't like. Ask him to describe the tastes and textures he's experiencing as he eats. Help him regulate the speed with which he eats. Suggest that he set his utensils down in between bites. Make sure he swallows fully and maybe takes a sip of beverage every few bites. Being a great role model in the kitchen and at the table is one of the best ways to help.

How You Can Ease the Food Transition

Make familiar foods. Robin's husband loved preparing congee for their daughter, who loved this Chinese rice porridge.

Don't rush your child off the bottle. Part of the bonding process involves feeding, and bottle-feeding is one of the ways to create that bond. Bottle-feeding can be a very special time, one that your child may not have experienced. So, there's no rush to wean your older infant or young toddler off a bottle. Make sure to clean your child's teeth after the last bottle before bedtime.

Make eating fun. While preparing and serving meals to children can sometimes be stressful for any family, try to make it really enjoyable for your newly adopted child. Create a light atmosphere in the kitchen. Always take your cues from your child. If he's in the mood, play music or dance while you make dinner. For an older child, allow him to help with food selection, preparation, and service. Set the table in a fun way—use colorful plates or napkins. Allow him to be creative with designing the way food is presented (eg, in the shape of a face or an animal). For a younger child, get messy. Encourage him to put his fingers into food, smell food before it goes into his mouth, lick his fingers, and explore textures. Laugh with your child, so he knows this is OK. Don't worry, because this behavior will not last and as you model appropriate adult eating behaviors, he will learn good habits.

Offer healthy options. Have healthy snacks available that older children can get on their own. Create a special place where your child knows that food is always available. You can place a tray that contains yogurts, cheese sticks, hummus, and cut-up vegetables into your refrigerator. You can also designate a certain cabinet or shelf or a certain lunch box in your kitchen where your child can always find nutritional snacks.

Common feeding questions

Q: What's the best formula for my baby?

A: I generally don't recommend specific brands of baby formula. Most baby formulas are quite similar. Your pediatrician will make recommendations based on your child's age and nutritional status.

Q: My child is hoarding food. What do I do?

A: If you think your child is hoarding food, please reassure him that food is plentiful in your house. Make a space in your kitchen—maybe in a cabinet or a spot in the refrigerator or in his own special lunch box—where he can go for "his" food. If you find food in your child's room, under his bed or in his closet, don't scold him. Have him help you clean up any mess, and remind him where food is in the house and how he can access it.

When you and your child are ready, go to the grocery store together and let him make some independent choices around food selection. Let him unpack the groceries at home and then put his food in his designated place in the kitchen.

Bathing

Some children love the bath, and others don't. It may be a new or different experience from what happened in a child's previous caregiving situation. Try to make bath time as pleasant an experience as possible. If taking a bath really upsets your child, give him a sponge bath or clean him with a washcloth instead. Give him fun bath toys to splash around in a smaller bucket of water. Remember that bathrooms can be noisy with echoing sound. And you might want to get in the bathtub with him. If you have other children, you may want him to watch the other children bathe first.

Robin remembers...

My daughter didn't like the first bath we gave her. That may have been because the water was too cold! Even my husband yelped when I made him get into the bathtub. What a rookie parenting mistake—I was worried that the water would be too hot and burn her, so I ran it too cold. Not surprisingly, it took a while for her to like the bath. But once she did, she splashed and played for hours. Getting her out was the hard part!

Common bathing questions

Q: Should I get into the bathtub with my toddler?

A: Getting into the bathtub is your call. For children who've never been in a bathtub before, this might be a good idea. Toddlers can be very active in a bathtub and, for this reason, more susceptible to injuries. It's tough to catch a wet 2-year-old!

Q: Is it OK for my child to bathe with my other children?

A: Check with your pediatrician first. If your child is at risk of intestinal parasites, you'll want your child to bathe alone until you know he's not going to infect anyone else in the family. While you don't need to wear gloves when you diaper or clean him, you don't want other children drinking bathwater if he has an accident.

Q: My child told me that he showered by himself in his foster home. Is that OK?

A: Even if your child seems old enough to shower alone, you'll want to gently supervise at first. Why? You want to make sure he knows what he's doing. Second, you will want to provide the nurturing around bathing that he may have never had. Handing him a towel, helping him dry his hair, and maybe applying moisturizer can all be wonderful bonding experiences.

Keep in mind, however, as tough as this is to think about, it's possible that your child was physically or sexually abused, and experiences such as bathing may be attached to some scary memories. If you notice unusual behaviors or suspect that something's not quite right, talk with your pediatrician immediately.

Toileting

Assume that whatever you've been told about your child's toileting habits will change. Any disruption or stress may show itself through his bladder or his gut, either during the day or at night. A younger child may struggle when you put a diaper on him, especially if he has never worn one before. Older children who are reportedly toilet-trained may need to wear diapers or training pants (eg, Pull-Ups). These children may be acting out, or displaying regressive behavior, or perhaps they were never really toilet-trained. Children may also start to wet the bed or have nighttime accidents. Don't worry, your child will figure this routine out, and you can help by going back to the beginning and teaching. Please be patient if your child regresses. He has to learn a new routine. Again, use reassuring language and make toileting a low-stress event.

Sibling Rivalry

If you have other children, their lives have also been turned upside down with your family's new addition. Even though you may have been preparing your children for months, the sibling order has changed. Your children may not take so well that the youngest may not be the youngest anymore, or there's a new child in the middle, who has different needs. Once the excitement of your addition has worn off, your other children may return to acting like typical children. No one can be on his best behavior all the time. You may hear feelings of resentment. You may see behaviors such as hitting and biting that you've never seen before. You may see an older sibling assume a "parent" role. A sibling may also express some excessive worry about a new sibling—when in fact he could be worrying about himself, and whether your love for him is still the same, now that he's sharing you with someone else.

Welcoming a new child to your family is not just about the new child. Each of your children wants to feel special and loved by you. Please spend quality time with each child. If your child feels better about himself, he will feel better about helping you. Show your children how they can take care of their new sibling in age-appropriate ways.

Remembering to Take Care of You

When you bring a new child into your home, it's easy to forget to take time for you. Parenting is a 24/7 job, and as a new parent, you need to replenish yourself. It's easy to put your child's needs ahead of your own. But then you may feel exhausted or frustrated and feel that you lack the creativity or flexibility you need as a parent.

Please eat right and rest when your child naps or sleeps. Find ways to slow down and clear your head—whether it's exercise, reading, knitting, or mindfulness meditation. You need to restore your energy so you can care for your child. Don't forget to ask your family and friends for the help you need, particularly with the everyday household tasks that can mount and feel overwhelming.

Making the Transition

As one of my families used to say, "Nothing means anything until 3 weeks after the adoption." Don't take your child's behavior personally as he adjusts to his new home. Please give your new family time to settle in. As all of you make the transition, pay attention to anything that causes you particular stress or to certain behaviors you notice that concern you. Keep track by writing them down or making notes in your phone. You're headed to the pediatrician soon, and she will listen and offer support.

CHAPTER 3

Your Child's First Pediatric Visit: A Comprehensive Health Evaluation

Lisa and Matthew couldn't wait to introduce their 12-month-old bundle of joy to their pediatrician, Dr Martin, who specialized in adoption medicine. They had met with her for a pre-adoption consultation before their trip to Taiwan to meet their daughter, and she had reviewed the medical information the couple had received. Now they were excited to show Audrey off.

Dr Martin couldn't have been calmer, kinder, and more reassuring during their child's first visit. But baby Audrey was terrified. Seeing Dr Martin in her white coat, Audrey started to cry. Maybe she remembered an unpleasant experience with a doctor or nurse poking and prodding her. Audrey's anxiety only compounded Lisa and Matthew's own. They couldn't stand seeing their daughter so upset and were worried about what the doctor might discover. There were a lot of tests being conducted on their little girl!

— *Lisa and Matthew, parents to*
12-month-old Audrey

I don't mean to scare you with Lisa and Matthew's story, but few children "love" going to the physician. Your child's first medical examination may cause both of you more anxiety because your child is adopted. Please know your physician is there to help with the medical examination as well as the emotions and anxiety that may swirl for your child and for you. In this chapter, I explain what will happen at your child's first visit, why your physician will conduct such a comprehensive examination, and how your child might feel so you can feel prepared walking into the examination room.

A comprehensive post-adoption evaluation, whether you adopted internationally or domestically, is essential. The American Academy of Pediatrics (AAP) recommends scheduling your child's first appointment to occur in the first few weeks after bringing your child home. At this visit, your pediatrician will review your child's history—including any existing medical diagnoses; screen for any unrecognized medical issues; and evaluate developmental and behavioral concerns. (If you have adopted a newborn, you will, of course, go right away and follow the newborn schedule for well-child visits [also called *health supervision visits*].) If you adopted internationally, the medical information you have may be limited and inaccurate, and you may have very little or no information about prenatal care or birth circumstances. If you adopted a new-born domestically, you may have more-detailed background medical history, and your newborn will probably have had all necessary tests performed in the nursery before discharge. With foster care adoption, there may be more gaps in your child's health history, and your child may or may not have had appropriate screenings. Your pediatrician will try to fill in the blanks and determine which tests are necessary.

At this first visit, your pediatrician reviews the past medical history, assesses development, and discusses feeding, sleeping, and behavioral issues. You may be most concerned about whether your child is adjusting well to you and to her new environment, and your pediatrician can answer questions about your transition as a family. Your pediatrician will also conduct a full medical examination of your child and perform screening blood work to evaluate your child's nutritional status and check for infectious diseases. It's crucial that the pediatrician check for any outward manifestation of disease as well as conditions that may not be so obvious, such as anemia, lead poisoning, and parasitic infections. Adopted children

Before the First Office Visit

Here's what you can do before leaving for the pediatric office to help calm you and your child.

- Bring food, such as a bottle for an infant or a sippy cup and snacks for a toddler.

- Bring stuffed animals or toys, or any object that might provide comfort.

- Collect all your documents the night before the appointment. Remember your list of questions, and bring a pen and pad to take notes or make sure your phone is charged.

- Be prepared to wait. If you can, try to schedule the first morning or afternoon appointment to minimize waiting.

- Help your child prepare by reading her a developmentally appropriate book about a pediatric visit.

- Talk about what will happen at the pediatric office, since it's a new place, with new people and new smells/ sights/sounds.

- If an older child asks about blood tests or injections (shots), please be honest, even if your answer makes her anxious. Plan something fun to look forward to after the visit. (Please don't reward your child with candy during the examination.)

are more at risk for infectious diseases, malnutrition, and problems caused by environmental exposures. Of course, if your child is sick upon your return home, bring her to your physician immediately.

First Examination Jitters for You and Your Child

Be prepared for a long and overwhelming first visit. The pediatrician will have many questions for you, and you may have many questions for her.

Questions Your Pediatrician Will Ask You at Your Child's First Visit

- How are things going?
- Do you have any concerns about her health?
- What's the daily routine like?
- How is your child feeding and sleeping?
- What's her toileting routine like?
- How would you describe her personality?
- How do you feel attachment and bonding are coming along?

Most important, she's going to ask you about *your* concerns, so come prepared with a list of questions.

It's likely to be an emotionally stressful and draining experience for you and your child. Your pediatrician will know this and will do her best to comfort your child—and you. She will listen very carefully to your concerns. She may offer to check in with you in a few days to see how things are going or to provide you with some parent handouts that help you understand any medical information that she's shared. Someone from her office may call with laboratory test results.

When the pediatrician starts to examine your child, try to relax! She knows how to observe and examine your child. She will warm her hands and stethoscope before placing either one on your child's skin. She will find ways to engage and connect with your child. It may be, though, that your child is too scared and no matter what the pediatrician does, your child will howl and cling to you. Don't worry. Your pediatrician experiences this sort of reaction regularly. She will not think any less of you, as a parent, or think negatively about your child. Over time, all of you will get to know each other and trust the relationship.

Make sure to bring to the first post-adoption appointment any additional medical information you may have received, such as an immunization booklet. If your child joined your family through international adoption, she underwent a physician's examination at a US-approved medical facility in the country of adoption to finish her paperwork. Bring those documents as well. Perhaps you also learned more about your child's prenatal history or her life in the orphanage, foster care, or her living environment. There will be many unknowns and limited information, so make sure to share any new information with your pediatrician.

This first visit also provides a baseline for your child's growth and future development. Many adopted children experience a period of catch-up growth, during which, with proper caregiving and nutrition, there's an acceleration of weight gain and height growth. If your child is adopted from foster care, she is at risk of developing obesity; if so, your pediatrician will provide guidance around weight management. Your pediatrician will start documenting developmental milestones and follow these on an ongoing basis.

Your pediatrician will recommend how often your child needs to be seen going forward. Future follow-up visits let your pediatrician assess growth and development, review laboratory test results, and catch your child up on any needed immunizations. As noted earlier, the visit frequency for domestically adopted newborns will be similar to the AAP recommended well-child schedule. For internationally adopted children and children adopted from foster care, the follow-up visits will be determined with your child's age and specific circumstances. As you and your child continue to adjust to life together as a family and establish more routines, you will be able to share more observations and anecdotes with your pediatrician and use her as the valuable resource she is.

Growth Measurements

Sasha was 18 months of age when she arrived from Ukraine. She was so small! Her height and weight weren't even on the growth curve. She ate like crazy for the first few weeks, and then she slowed down. She started throwing food from her high chair, instead of shoveling it into her mouth! We noticed that her onesies started becoming difficult to snap. Her pant legs seemed to shorten. She was growing! When we went to our pediatrician 6 months later, our pediatrician said Sasha was "on the curve for height and weight" and she was "catching up" appropriately.

— Maya and Don, watching their daughter grow

As part of the comprehensive physical examination, your pediatrician will take weight and height measurements as well as measure your child's head circumference. (Head circumference is tracked to see how the brain is growing.) These measurements are important to establish a baseline from which to follow your child's rate of growth once she is home. The pediatrician is prepared for a spurt of catch-up growth and development, given improved nutrition, comfort, and social interaction. After about a 6- to 9-month period, your pediatrician expects a child to "settle in" to a steady rate of growth.

Your pediatrician will plot measurements on the standard growth charts, recommended by the AAP. It's not so important where your child "sits" on the growth curve right now. It's important to track the velocity of growth over time. Remember, this is a starting point. If there are delays, there's likely to be catch-up growth, both physically and developmentally. Your pediatrician will track your child's growth over the next few years to see how your child is progressing. If your child is not displaying catch-up growth, your pediatrician will need to understand why and may need to perform more laboratory tests.

You might wonder whether country-specific growth charts should be used. Typically, pediatricians will not use these because they do not represent the way children living in orphanages grow.

Physical Examination

Your physician will examine your child head to toe. She will be sensitive as she approaches and begins to touch your child. She will listen to her heart and lungs, palpate her belly, and examine her genitalia. She will check the skin for any evidence of rashes and skin infections such as impetigo and scabies. She will take note of any scars and birthmarks. Darker-skinned children may have pigmented lesions known as *mongolian spots* or *congenital dermal melanocytosis* on their backs and bottoms, and these should be noted in the medical record so as not to be mistaken for bruises. The physician will look for any unusual physical findings that might indicate a syndrome, particularly facial features that might indicate fetal alcohol spectrum disorder. She will check for swelling in the neck as a possible indication of thyroid disease and swelling of the lymph nodes as a possible indication of tuberculosis (TB). The physician will examine your child's head, check her ears for signs of previous or current infections, perform an eye and nose examination, and get a good look inside her mouth for signs of tooth decay. Be sure to mention any physical concerns to your physician before she starts the examination.

Sometimes, it can be very challenging to complete the physical examination because your child may be too scared to cooperate. If so, your job, as a parent, is to let your child know that it's OK to be scared. Remind her that it's the physician's job to make sure she's healthy, and it's your job to keep her safe.

Your physician will know how best to position your child for the examination. If your child is an infant, your physician will probably examine her on the examination table. If your child is a toddler or preschooler, your physician will probably have your child sit on your lap. An older child may be comfortable on the examination table or may want to sit next to you or on your lap. Your physician may give your child a choice of where she would like to be examined to give her some sense of control.

She may also ask your child if it's OK to look inside her mouth, feel her belly, and perform other actions as she conducts the physical examination. This step may sound strange to you, but the physician wants to let your child know that she has choices about who touches her body as well as let your child create some personal boundaries. Keep in mind that prior to their adoption, many children were never given choices about a physical examination. And, more important, it's possible a child may have been physically or sexually abused, which may have created some confusion about who is allowed to touch the child and what type of touch is OK.

Laboratory Tests

If Audrey didn't like the poking and prodding during her physical examination, she—and I—had no idea of what was coming next. Dr Martin had to test Audrey's blood to see what, if any, vaccinations and illnesses she had had. We held her while she screamed. I worried that if Audrey wriggled too much we'd have to do the procedure again. Audrey and I both cried. I was stunned at how much blood was needed. I didn't realize how many screening tests were necessary.

> — *Lisa, recalling the extent of the post-adoption evaluation*

While a blood test is painful and scary, the AAP recommends that your physician obtain blood for certain tests on the basis of your adopted child's risk. For all adopted children born outside the United States, tests that were completed in the country of birth should be repeated according to US recommendations. That's why your physician conducts comprehensive blood tests and may have to draw so much blood. Although you may have your child's medical and immunization records, you can't be sure how accurate or complete they were.

At this first visit, your physician will order a number of laboratory tests, including a complete blood cell count, a comprehensive metabolic panel, a thyroid function test, and a lead level test. She may also order blood tests to assess the quality and accuracy of vaccinations your child may have previously been given. If this sounds like a lot of blood, it is! But your physician needs all this information to evaluate your child's overall health.

All adopted children are at risk of being undernourished. A complete blood cell count is used to check for anemia. Your child may need to take vitamins with some form of iron supplementation for

Post-adoption Evaluation the Physician Should Perform for Growth and Nutritional Issues

- Measure length, height, weight (unclothed), and head circumference (for all children). Use standard CDC or WHO growth charts to determine growth percentiles.

- Growth should be monitored and further workup done if there is not catch-up growth by 6 months after arrival in the home.

- Check CBC to evaluate for anemia and blood disorders. Hemoglobin electrophoresis should be done for children at risk for some types of red blood cell diseases.

- Check lead level for environmental risks.

- Check thyrotropin level (in some countries, the soil is deficient of iodine).

- Check newborn screening panel (young infants).

Abbreviations: CBC, complete blood cell count; CDC, Centers for Disease Control and Prevention; WHO, World Health Organization.

Adapted from American Academy of Pediatrics. Internationally adopted children: important information for parents. HealthyChildren.org. https://www.healthychildren.org/English/family-life/family-dynamics/adoption-and-foster-care/Pages/Internationally-Adopted-Children-Important-Information-for-Parents.aspx. Updated November 1, 2017. Accessed May 11, 2018.

a while. A comprehensive metabolic panel provides information about how the kidneys and liver are functioning, including vitamin D status. Your child may need to take vitamin D supplements. Your physician will also screen for infectious diseases such as TB, syphilis, hepatitis A, hepatitis B, hepatitis C, and HIV infection.

For internationally adopted children, additional tests may be added to screen for infectious diseases endemic to the country your child is from.

All internationally adopted children will also need to have their stools checked for parasites. The physician will provide the kits for stool collection or will send you to the laboratory to pick up the stool containers. Instructions for stool collection are usually included in the kits. (Don't worry! It's pretty easy to do this, particularly if your child is still in diapers or training pants [eg, Pull-Ups].)

Vaccinations and Immunizations

At the first visit, your physician may suggest "starting from the beginning," as if your child has never received immunizations. This is the best way to keep your child protected from vaccine-preventable diseases. Even if your child received some injections (shots) or extra shots—as is often the case for children adopted internationally or from foster care—most vaccines can be repeated safely. Or, after looking at your child's immunization records, your physician may decide to administer some vaccines and also use laboratory tests that screen for the presence of antibodies that will help determine immunity. These results will help your physician decide how to schedule catch-up immunizations at future visits.

Some vaccines may need to be administered for the first time. Some internationally adopted children may not have received vaccines for chickenpox, *Haemophilus influenzae* type b, pneumococcal bacteria, and influenza. Children need to be vaccinated according to the US schedule. This vaccination is not only important for your adopted child but also important for your family members and friends. There have been reports of people who have been exposed to newly adopted children and have contracted vaccine-preventable diseases such as measles.

It's also a good idea to make sure all household members and any other people who will be in close contact with your child (such as child care providers and extended family members) are appropriately vaccinated against hepatitis A and hepatitis B. Adults should confirm that they have immunity to chickenpox and measles.

Finally, I always recommend that everyone gets a flu vaccine during flu season. As a new parent, you can't afford to get sick. Even if you "never get the flu," your child is susceptible to the flu. And remember to be prepared for the 8 to 10 viral infections that your child may have during her first winter!

Infectious Diseases

Your physician needs to test your child for certain infectious diseases, including hepatitis A, hepatitis B, hepatitis C, syphilis, TB, and HIV. This may seem daunting, but it is necessary. The AAP recommends repeating some of these tests (hepatitis B and C, TB, and HIV infection) 6 months later, even if the initial test results were negative, in case your child became infected shortly before she became part of your family.

Tuberculosis

It is important to screen your child for TB, which is prevalent in Eastern Europe, Latin America, and Africa. Russia, Eastern Europe, South Africa, and Asia also have high rates of multidrug-resistant TB. Children adopted from foster care are also at increased risk for TB, as they may have been exposed to family members who spent time in prison.

While active TB—the contagious type—does not show up often, a fair number of adopted children have latent TB in their blood. *Latent* means that the TB could turn into the illness. Latent TB is best to treat before it becomes active, and your child experiences the fever, the fatigue, the cough, and other symptoms associated with TB. If your child has latent TB, she will need to take medication

Post-adoption Testing the Physician Should Perform for Infectious Diseases

- TST or IGRA testing for TB. This should be done even if the child was immunized with the BCG vaccine. TST is preferred for children younger than 2 years.
- Hepatitis B virus serological testing: hepatitis B surface antigen (HBsAg), hepatitis B surface antibody (anti-HBs), and hepatitis B core antibody (anti-HBc).
- Hepatitis C virus serological testing.
- HIV serological testing.
- Syphilis serological testing: RPR or VDRL test, and FTA-ABS or TP-PA test.
- Stool examination for ova and parasites (3 recommended, best collected 48 hours apart), with specific request for *Giardia* and *Cryptosporidium* testing.
- Stool bacterial culture (if diarrhea present).
- Serological testing for other parasites and parasitic infections such as *Trypanosoma cruzi,* lymphatic filariasis, *Strongyloides* species, and also *Schistosoma* species for certain children.
- Evaluate immunization status by checking antibody titers for vaccines previously given (eg, diphtheria antibody titers, tetanus antibody titers, polio neutralizing titers) *or* repeat immunizations. (Exceptions may include children from foster homes in Korea.)

Abbreviations: FTA-ABS, fluorescent treponemal antibody absorption; IGRA, interferon-γ release assay; RPR, rapid plasma reagin; TB, tuberculosis; TP-PA, *Treponema pallidum* passive particle agglutination; TST, tuberculin skin test.

Adapted from American Academy of Pediatrics. Internationally adopted children: important information for parents. HealthyChildren.org. https://www.healthychildren.org/English/family-life/family-dynamics/adoption-and-foster-care/Pages/Internationally-Adopted-Children-Important-Information-for-Parents.aspx. Updated November 1, 2017. Accessed May 11, 2018.

for 9 months. See whether your pharmacy can mix the medication with a child-friendly flavor so the medication is more palatable.

Your physician will test your child for TB either with a blood test or using the TST (tuberculin skin test) injected just under the skin of the forearm. (This is not the 4-prong prick skin test that you may remember from childhood.) The TST may cause some redness and may cause a bump to form that can swell or harden. These temporary reactions are what the physician will assess when you bring your child back in 48 to 72 hours to have the test read.

If your child has a positive test result, she will have a chest x-ray to rule out active TB. Like getting a blood test or immunization, having an x-ray may be an intimidating and scary experience for your child. She will be alone and somewhat restrained, listening to loud machines. Ask whether you can be in the room to hold her hand and soothe her.

Your child may have a scar on her shoulder or on her upper back, suggesting that she received a vaccine for TB called *BCG*. Even if she has had a BCG vaccine, it does not provide long-term protection against TB. The AAP recommends testing all children who were previously vaccinated for TB. The AAP also recommends repeating TB testing 3 to 6 months after arrival, even if the initial test result is negative.

Lead Poisoning

All adopted children younger than 6 years are screened for lead poisoning. If your child is older and has a developmental delay, she should also be screened for lead poisoning. The most common source of lead is lead found in paint. Even though lead paint is no longer used in the United States, it can be found in other parts of the world. It is also used in jewelry and in pottery glaze. Lead can also be found in some ethnic food products and certain dyes that are placed on the skin. Your child may have been exposed prenatally or in her living environment. If undetected, lead poisoning can lead to brain damage, possibly affecting your child's behavior, academic achievement, ability to pay attention, and IQ.

If levels are high initially, it's likely from an orphanage environment. However, you will need to also check your home for lead—paint on doors and windowsills is often the culprit. Talk with your pediatrician about lead risk assessment resources in your area. Lead levels can be lowered with a diet high in calcium and iron and low in fat.

Hepatitis

Hepatitis A is a self-limited viral infection contracted through ingestion of food or water or when a child is in close contact with someone who has the infection. It's important to test for hepatitis A, because if your child is positive, she can infect others around her.

Children infected with *hepatitis B* or *C*—blood-borne viruses that can cause liver disease—often don't have any symptoms. If your child is diagnosed as having hepatitis B or C, your pediatrician will have you work with pediatric infectious disease specialists or pediatric gastroenterologists to help monitor and manage the infection. (See Chapter 5 for more information.)

Gastrointestinal Parasites

OK, collecting stool samples from your child isn't the most fun job! But it's important to screen for parasites that can contribute to your child's malnutrition. Your pediatrician will advise you when and how to collect the stool sample.

The most common parasite is *Giardia* species. These microscopic parasites are quite common in internationally adopted children. Young children with *Giardia* infection often don't exhibit symptoms, while older children may have diarrhea or tell you about abdominal pain. Fortunately, *Giardia* infection is usually easy to treat. After your child completes 7 to 10 days of medication, you'll need to do another stool collection. It's important to know that the infection has cleared.

Giardia infection is very contagious. Your child will not be able to go to child care or school if she's infected. If you have other children in your home, you'll want to keep them out of the bathtub when you are bathing your infected child. As long as everyone keeps their hands clean and out of their mouths, there shouldn't be a problem with others in your house becoming infected.

Important Appointments to Make

At your child's first appointment, make sure to ask your pediatrician about screening for vision and hearing and when to schedule a dental appointment. Ask for referrals and whether any of the subspecialists your pediatrician recommends has experience with adopted children. Early detection of any concerns can prevent difficulties later, as a child having a hard time hearing or seeing may have difficulties with speech and language or in the classroom. Children who have bleeding gums, or whose teeth appear rotted, or those who tell you about tooth pain should visit the dentist sooner rather than later.

Vision

Within a few months of arrival, try to bring your child to a pediatric ophthalmologist. The physician will check for strabismus, which is any misalignment of the eyes, including crossed eyes, as well as examine the eyes and pupil. Some children may experience excessive tearing or have eyelash or eyelid concerns.

Hearing

Undiagnosed or untreated ear infections could lead to hearing loss. That possibility means it's critical to do a routine check. (Note that newborns born in the United States are routinely screened at birth.)

Hearing is crucial to language development, and impaired hearing can lead to speech delays.

Oral Health

All adopted children, regardless of age at adoption, should be seen by a dentist. In addition, the American Dental Association recommends that a child's first dental visit should occur at the time of the eruption of the first tooth and no later than 12 months of age. A dental visit is crucial because of the potential lack of dental care. Many foreign countries and some parts of the United States lack fluoridated water. Ask your pediatrician about a fluoride varnish while you wait to get a dental appointment scheduled.

The dentist can check for tooth decay as well as progress in tooth eruption. Children are more likely to have inadequate enamel, which can lead to cavities, even in baby teeth.

Remember to start cleaning and healthy mouth-habits young. The American Dental Association recommends brushing baby teeth with fluoride toothpaste as soon as the first baby teeth appear.

Other Subspecialty Appointments

If your child has a medical condition that requires urgent attention, you may need to schedule an appointment with a pediatric subspecialist. Talk with your pediatrician about the timing of all these referrals and what's right for your child and your family. For example, you may need to see a pediatric cardiologist if your child was diagnosed as having congenital heart disease. If your child had been prescribed medications for mood disorders or attention challenges or has any mental health concerns, please get a referral to a pediatric psychologist or pediatric psychiatrist.

For children with a complex medical condition such as a cleft lip and palate or a myelomeningocele (the most serious form of spina bifida), future office visits may take place in the form of multidisciplinary clinics, where different subspecialists see your child during the same appointment. This appointment can be very overwhelming for you and your child. You can prepare yourself by getting a good night's rest the day before. Give yourself plenty of time to travel to the appointment. Bring a change of clothes (including extra diapers or underwear), food, toys, and anything that will comfort your child. Consider bringing a notebook with questions for all the physicians. It might be difficult to listen to all the information while you're trying to keep your child comfortable. Be sure to get the names and phone numbers of the physicians and nurses. Sometimes there's a particular person, such as a pediatric nurse practitioner, who will be your contact for future appointments and procedures. Ask the physician how best to communicate when you have concerns.

The Circumcision Decision

If you've adopted a young boy who's uncircumcised, you may wonder whether to have him circumcised. While the scientific evidence suggests that the health benefits of circumcision outweigh the risks, the American Academy of Pediatrics recommends that the decision to circumcise is best made by parents in consultation with their pediatrician, taking into account what is in the best interests of the child, including medical, religious, cultural, and ethnic traditions. Special considerations for an adopted child include the risk of general anesthesia and the potential trauma caused by the procedure itself. Some parents are concerned that their son won't look like other male members of the family or male peers. I explain that nobody looks exactly the same, even if they're related by blood! If you're interested in circumcision, ask your pediatrician for a referral to a pediatric surgeon or pediatric urologist.

Follow-up Visits

Now that the first pediatric visit is over, you will need a follow-up visit about 4 to 6 weeks later to review the laboratory work and blood test results. This follow-up appointment is a wonderful time to review how your child has been transitioning and what developmental and behavioral milestones she has reached. You've all had time to get settled in as a family, establish a sleep and eating schedule, and see how relationships are forming. Ask for advice about the newest member of your family.

> ## *Robin remembers...*
>
> I remember my doctor gently telling me at our child's first appointment that we weren't putting the diaper on tight enough, so it was remedial diapering for us! I would also bring a pink spiral notebook to every appointment, so I could write all my questions and my doctor's answers in one place. I still have that notebook, with my notes and observations, and the results from various specialist visits. And how can I ever forget my daughter biting the dentist at her first visit? I was mortified, but the dentist took it all in stride and we still go to her practice. I also asked my spouse to come to what appointments he could; I found having another adult with me helped immeasurably. Someone else could listen and remember the doctor's advice!

Managing the follow-up appointments may be challenging, so work with your physician to space out the appointments. If you need to see a subspecialist, consider timing the appointments to be the least disruptive to you and your child. If you need to schedule several appointments on the same day, try to take a break in between by getting something to eat or stepping outside for some fresh air. Your child will be exhausted—and so will you. Most important, make sure all the varied screenings are done so if there is a problem, you can be on top of it. The earlier you can evaluate, the earlier you can begin any needed interventions.

Now that you have a new person in your life, you have new responsibilities. Figure out how to organize medical and other information, as you will have appointments to keep track of, immunization records to maintain, and forms to complete for child care or school, plus potential paperwork related to the adoption. Many parents bring a folder or notebook with their child's medical records to their appointments with me. I also encourage the parents I work with to keep a running list of questions and observations in a notebook or on a phone so they remember what they want to share with me at their child's next visit.

Partnering With Your Pediatrician

You want reassurances from your pediatrician that all will be OK, but, of course, no one knows that for any child. You may feel unsure, now, because your pediatrician has raised more unknowns about your child's health history. There will always be unknowns and unanswered questions.

The good news is that your pediatrician is your partner. Together, you can watch for any short- or long-term consequences of your child's experiences before adoption. Your pediatrician will check for the typical physical and developmental childhood issues, but you both can remain cognizant of how your child's early life may be playing a role in her development. Your pediatrician will be a valuable resource for health issues you encounter now and throughout your child's development.

CHAPTER 4

Your Follow-up Visit: How Are Things Going?

I couldn't believe how well Jordan was adjusting. Even though he'd been in 3 foster homes before adoption, he seemed to be adjusting to our home. We were still having bouts of tears but not like we did during those first few days. Jordan had started to let me hold his hand when we walked into new places. He'd also started making better eye contact with me. And last night, he kissed me on the cheek when I put him to bed.

— Linda, mother of Jordan, aged 6 years

I look forward to the first follow-up visit with adopted families because there is typically so much positive change since our first appointment. By now, you have recovered from the shock of coming home. Your family has further adjusted to the rhythms of being a family together. Now I'd like to discuss your life as a family.

At this appointment, we have a chance to talk about more than the results of the laboratory tests.

My first questions to parents are "How are things going?" and "Do you have any new concerns, thoughts, or questions?" I know you want to know whether your child is OK. I also want to know whether you are OK. Often at this appointment, families open up about the emotional aspects of settling in. It's worth repeating that the first few weeks and months can be bumpy.

Of course, if any medical issues have arisen since your child's first visit, you will have called your pediatrician. If your pediatrician hasn't heard from you, she will probably assume all has been fine health-wise.

Your pediatrician will start the office visit by addressing your concerns, and then she will take a detailed history about what's happened over the past 4 to 6 weeks. She will ask about any new illnesses, developmental progression, feeding patterns and behaviors, sleeping habits, and, most important, how bonding and family adjustment is going in general as well as specifically in regards to relationships with (if relevant) siblings, other extended family members, and child care providers. She will also review laboratory test results and discuss what, if any, immunizations are needed.

Seeing the Pediatrician

In my experience, most adopted children returning for a second visit are scared to some degree, no matter the child's age. Younger children scream, or cry, or shut down. An older child's body language often says it all.

When Your Child Is Scared

Your child may be reluctant to come back to the pediatric office—and that's fine. I expect your child to be scared. Why? He may remember how he felt at the previous visit. He may recall the strange loud noises of elevators or pagers. He may remember being poked and prodded by a number of people—maybe in white coats or not. He no doubt experienced physical pain with blood tests and injections (shots). Being afraid of a physician, or hospital, or medical situation, is a perfectly normal response.

When Your Child Is Not Scared

What if your child doesn't appear to be scared? Don't worry. This behavior isn't an immediate cause for alarm. Your pediatrician may ask you how you and your child are bonding. Does your child get upset when he hurts himself? Does he seek your comfort when he's scared or in pain? It may be that your child has an amazingly high pain threshold or that he's taking his time to work out how he feels about himself or you (or himself and you). Children will regulate

---

Providing Your Child's Immunization Records

As your child enters licensed child care or school, you will have to submit an immunization record that documents proof of protection from vaccine-preventable diseases. This requirement is to protect your child and all children and caregivers in the child care or school environment. Don't be alarmed if you receive a note indicating that your child needs "more vaccines" or is "behind on immunizations." Your pediatrician can write a letter to explain that your child is in the process of catch-up immunizations or has serological or "blood" immunity (proven by a blood test) to a particular vaccine-preventable disease and is considered age appropriately immunized.

---

their own trust "barometer" by referring to their prior experiences with attachment (see Chapter 6) and your reactions as a parent.

Preparing for Your Follow-up Visit

You can help by talking with your child before the office visit, reminding him that the physician's job is to help him be healthy. The blood tests and shots are painful and scary, but they are necessary and usually quick. If your child can understand, ask him how you can help him feel OK. Would he like to sit on your lap? Would he like to bring a special toy, or stuffed animal, or a comfort item to the visit? Consider taking a picture of your physician and showing it to your child several times before the visit so he can remember what his physician looks like. And remember that your physician won't take any behavior personally. After all, who among us likes getting shots?

Laboratory Test Results

Even if you've already received your child's laboratory test results by phone or via electronic health records, your pediatrician will probably review these results again. Your pediatrician will want to make sure you understand the interpretation and give you an opportunity to ask questions. If antibody titers were measured to determine whether your child needs additional immunizations, your pediatrician will be able to give you a projected immunization schedule, which may include immunizations at this visit. If your child is capable of understanding, you may want to let him know that he might have to get some more shots at this visit. Sometimes I start this visit by answering this question first, as I know it's usually the only concern the child has on his mind.

If your child is younger than 12 months or had a questionable immunization record, your pediatrician may have started the vaccine series from the beginning. Your pediatrician will follow the Centers for Disease Control and Prevention recommendations for catch-up immunizations. Keep in mind that some older children will not need to be vaccinated against *Haemophilus influenzae* type b or *Streptococcus pneumoniae* (pneumococcus) because vaccines designed to prevent these diseases are intended to protect very young children. Remember, vaccines are one of the best developments in preventive medicine. Vaccines are safe and effective.

Catch-up Growth

When Your Child Is Growing as Fast as Expected

Most children experience catch-up growth, thanks to improved nutrition and care. Parents are often amazed by how much their child changes physically in the time since the previous visit. I often hear "He's grown right out of his pants. See how much shorter they are!" Your pediatrician will take new growth measurements to see how your child's physical growth is progressing. We want to track height and weight and, if your child is younger than 2 years, head circumference.

When Your Child Is Not Growing as Fast as Expected

Sometimes, however, growth is slower than it should be or hasn't taken off. If there hasn't been adequate weight gain, your pediatrician will ask about nutrition and feeding patterns. "Is your child drinking water instead of milk? Is he a picky eater or an adventurous one? Is he having regular snacks?"

If your child is growing slower than expected, it may be time to recheck for parasites, so be prepared to collect more stool samples. Once again, follow your pediatrician's directions on when and how to collect samples. Your pediatrician may also test for *Helicobacter pylori* bacteria, which can cause peptic ulcer disease. *H pylori* infections are more common in children adopted from developing countries. Symptoms may include appetite or weight loss, bloating, burping, and nausea. Your pediatrician will order a blood test or collect a stool sample to test for *H pylori*.

Gastroesophageal reflux disease (GERD) can also cause poor feeding and slow weight gain. GERD causes inflammation of your child's esophagus, which can make eating uncomfortable. Symptoms can include bad breath, burping, heartburn or chest pain, and food refusal. Avoiding fatty and fried foods can help, and medications are available. If dietary modifications and medication don't help, your pediatrician may refer you to a pediatric gastroenterologist who has specialized training in problems of the gastrointestinal tract.

Your pediatrician can also screen for celiac disease and cystic fibrosis. Celiac disease is an allergy to gluten, and the inflammation caused might prevent needed nutrients from being absorbed by your child's body, leading to poor growth. Cystic fibrosis is an inherited condition that causes damage to the lungs, the digestive system, and other body organs.

Other Physical Changes You May Notice in Your Child

Changes in nutrition may lead to other physical changes. Parents frequently tell me that they notice

- They are trimming their child's nails more frequently.
- Their child's hair is thicker and more filled in.
- There is a change in their child's hair texture.
- The feel of their child's skin has changed—it feels healthy, not dry and doughy.
- Sometimes, skin tone has improved, and their child doesn't look as pale as he used to be.

Make sure to tell your pediatrician if you see any of these changes or other ones you've noticed.

Finally, your child may be refusing to eat because his teeth hurt or his mouth hurts. Your child may have weak enamel, causing sensitivities to hot and cold foods or liquids, or he may have undetected cavities. If so, your pediatrician may refer you to a pediatric dentist.

Feeding Issues

You may have noticed a shift from your child eating constantly during the first 2 weeks home to now not wanting to eat anymore or forgetting to eat. Don't be too surprised! This shift often happens because your child has figured out how to be full. He may also be acting like a typical toddler, who thinks: *Why sit and eat when I could be moving about? There are more interesting things to explore and do at home!*

Feeding Preferences

Your child is also developing feeding preferences. You are now serving him a wider range of tastes, textures, and flavors. So, now he might be more selective about what he wants to eat. If your child is old enough, allow him to help with meal preparation and setting the table. Consider offering choices at every meal. You don't want to offer too many choices, however. Keep it simple. "Do you want your broccoli on a plate or in a bowl?" "Do you want apple slices or applesauce?" "Do you want to dip your carrots in hummus or yogurt?"

Sensory Challenges Around Food

Beyond nutritional or physical reasons for too little weight gain, some children have sensory challenges around food. Depending on their previous living environments, they may have experienced some inappropriate feeding techniques, such as bottle propping and forced feeding. As a result, they didn't develop the ability to swallow or chew their food properly. Your pediatrician may refer your child to an occupational therapist or a feeding therapist.

Anxiety About Eating

Your child might also feel anxious about eating. He may still worry about where his next meal is coming from, as he is still operating from a survival perspective. Consider that mealtime may not have been as loving and pleasant as it is now, so your child needs to learn how to interact during family mealtime. Even the eye contact and expectation of engaging with others may be stressful. If mealtime is stressful, take a step back and slow things down. You may need to reintroduce various foods slowly, or you may need to feed your child as if he's a little younger than he really is.

Your Child Feeding Himself

From a developmental angle, all children must figure out how to feed themselves. Your child may not have learned that skill or may have only rudimentary skills with utensils. Once your child is a young toddler, you will have to teach him how to use a fork or spoon.

Some younger children may have trouble with feeding, as they didn't learn how to feed themselves properly in their respective prior care situations. Talk with your pediatrician if your child has difficulty drinking from a bottle or cup or has trouble chewing and swallowing. You might also notice a tongue-thrust action, or your child may drool excessively because of some low muscle-tone issues. Your child might need the help of a speech and language therapist to learn to control the muscles that help him chew and swallow.

Sleeping Issues

We'd set up a room for J. T. all for himself. He'd always had to share a bed in his foster homes. We bought him his own race-car bed, with matching sheets. We put sports decals on the walls. We didn't understand why he hated to go to bed. About 30 minutes before bedtime, he would start to get all worked up, and it would take him hours to fall asleep. He kept leaving the room and sneaking into his brother's bed next door.

— Chris and Riley, parents to J. T. and Tyrell, both adopted from foster care

Sleeping issues may take longer to smooth out, as many children, adopted or not, sometimes don't want to separate from their parents. They may have anxiety about the dark or going to sleep. Preschoolers, in particular, might think there's a monster under the bed or be afraid of being alone at night. I like to ask families how much has changed in the evening routine—what has improved and what hasn't. Talk with your child about nighttime fears. Instead of joking about the monster under the bed, acknowledge the fear and offer reassurance and support.

Sometimes, families see dramatic changes: you don't have to sleep in your child's room anymore, or your son looks forward to his evening routine. Transitions to sleep may be better. I like to remind parents that bedtime is a process that usually begins with a bath, is followed by reading books, and concludes with some downtime of cuddling and talking. Even though you may be ready for a quick "Good night," your child may need more time to slow down and transition to separating from you. It can take your child 30 minutes to an hour sometimes to fall asleep. It doesn't happen the moment his head hits the pillow!

I'll also talk with families about where they ultimately want a child to sleep. Some children are content being in their own beds in a room by themselves, right from the beginning. Other children need to be with their parents for a while.

> *We finally gave in and let J. T. sleep in his brother's room. We explained to him that he was going to sleep with Tyrell, and there was to be no fooling around. The first night, it was as if he was a different child. Both boys giggled for a few minutes, and then they were fast asleep. We realized that J. T. was probably scared to be alone, and all the things in his new room weren't helping him feel comfortable.*
>
> — *Chris and Riley, on how they smoothed out sleeping issues*

If your child is not ready to sleep where you want him to sleep, make the transition slowly. Think about what may have felt comfortable and safe in his prior sleeping environment, and adapt to this setup. Maybe you need to sleep in his room with him, for a while—even if that wasn't your plan. During the day, have your child play in the room where you want him to sleep. Help him feel secure.

Developmental and Behavioral Concerns

The follow-up visit is also a good time to check in with your pediatrician about any developmental and behavioral concerns. Some delays are to be expected, considering your child's age and pre-adoption care. Your child may not have experienced enough stimulation, physical contact, and nurturing.

Now that he's with you and more used to being part of a family, you may have already noticed developmental progress in the 4 to 6 weeks you've been together. While this improvement feels wonderful, it's important to discuss all progress with your pediatrician. Internationally adopted children and children adopted from foster care are at increased risk for developmental delays and behavioral challenges. It's better to get help earlier than later to improve future outcomes.

Assessing What's Going On

At 4 to 6 weeks home, I find, for the most part, that it is still too early to use standard developmental and behavioral screenings. Most screening tests are based on parent recall and your child's history, and we don't have a lot to go on yet. How effective an assessment will be also depends on the age of your child and what you are screening for.

We discuss speech and language therapy in Chapter 8 because it would be unusual to refer a child at the first follow-up visit. However, sometimes a parent observes that there has been no change in a child's sound production. Or, the parent notes that the child isn't catching on—that is, his receptive language (ie, what he understands) isn't improving. Those delays would be red flags. If you observe either delay, be sure your pediatrician checks for hearing or sends your child for an audiological consultation. (If your child is very young, it's impossible to perform hearing screening in the office.)

Movement Progress

Your pediatrician will ask you about your child's gross motor skills—his ability to sit, crawl, walk, run, and jump, depending on his age. Gross motor skills generally improve quickly and without intervention. But if you notice your child having trouble, make sure to mention it to a pediatrician. Your child may have low muscle tone caused by his pre-adoption circumstances. A physical therapist or an occupational therapist can help. You could also enroll your child in gym classes or swim classes and model play behavior on the playground or at home.

Robin remembers...

Our daughter would cruise around our apartment, holding on to the couch, the coffee table, and other furniture for balance. She moved around but would not walk by herself. I was concerned, so I mentioned this behavior at my follow-up visit to our adoption medical specialist. She, of course, reassured me that our daughter would walk when she was ready to. And what happened the next day? When David and I took her to the park, we sat down in the grass to play with her. She stood up, gave me a look, and walked easily from my lap to David, who was 10 feet away. Her expression said it all: *Of course, I can walk, silly Mommy!*

Your child will also be progressing with fine motor skills, although these can be a little more challenging. Depending on his age, is he using a utensil? How does he manipulate toys? Can he use a pencil or child-safe scissors if older? Is he learning to dress himself and brush his teeth? You may have to teach your child these basic skills. Ask your pediatrician for guidance.

Speech and Language Progress

Your pediatrician will also inquire about your child's speech and language progress. For internationally adopted children, are you hearing more and more English? Is your child still using his native language? What kinds of sounds does he make? How many words does he have? Does he recognize his name?

Again, it's tricky to test for delays this soon. However, as we discuss in Chapter 8, adopted children are more at risk for learning disabilities and speech and language concerns or delays. For internationally adopted kids, English is often their second language. Depending on your child's first living situation—orphanage or foster home—and the age of your child, he has learned varying degrees of his native language.

Domestically adopted newborns need to be followed closely, particularly if there were any suspicions of illicit substance use prenatally, even cigarette use. Children from foster care are also at risk of language delays, because of potential prenatal exposure to alcohol or drugs, genetic makeup, or trauma before adoption.

Please start the conversation now with your pediatrician so you both can keep it in front of you.

Behavioral Changes

Many parents remark that their child's behavior has changed significantly in the past 4 to 6 weeks, particularly regarding how he interacts with any primary caregivers. One dad commented: "Joey isn't climbing into my lap anymore or clinging to my leg. What's happening?" As children get more comfortable in their home environments, they may act more independent, which is what I hope will happen.

However, there's no one right way for a child to adjust, and you may have noticed different phases in this 4- to 6-week period and may notice them in the months to come. Your child may still feel extremely anxious around strangers, and that feeling might not dissipate for a while. I encourage parents to talk with their child about how he is feeling and provide a reassuring response.

Please remember that your child came to you fearful, anxious, and unsure of what was coming next. He likely had experienced instability and inconsistency. He needs to unlearn that and learn that you are there for him. He needs warmth, structure, and your parental sensitivity. He needs you to be highly involved in his emotional life. He will learn to trust and love.

Some parents note that their child isn't as "overly friendly" as he used to be. Some kids don't have a good social filter and will flit from person to person to try to seek attention. At first, this seems like a great social skill, but if you look at what's really happening, you'll realize that this behavior is not in his best interest. Children who depend on these superficial brief interactions are not developing friendly relationships with others. They may not make great eye contact with these strangers nor have any meaningful conversation. I want your child to learn to rely on you for comfort. You need to become his go-to person. If your child demonstrates this behavior, try to limit the number of outside contacts for a while. Use language about safety and strangers. Demonstrate some self-soothing techniques, such as rocking a baby doll or comforting your pet.

Always remember the age of your child and his adoption history. And remember the stages of development: a typical toddler will walk away from you yet look back to make sure you are there as his base.

Chapter 6 delves into attachment in more detail.

Transition to Child Care or School

For many families, parents have to return to their regular work schedules after 4 to 6 weeks at home. You've made your child care plan, and you have either gradually transitioned your child into child care or school (depending on your child's age) or brought a sitter into your home. What's this transition going to mean for you?

New adoptive parents, like all new parents, have mixed emotions about leaving their child with someone else so they can return to work. You may feel relieved or anxious. Some new parents struggle with the day-to-day child care work—changing diapers, frequent feedings, constant laundry, and other caregiving. This feeling is normal, particularly if you are the type of person who has thrived in a work environment. Being at home with a young child can feel socially isolating. You may miss the intellectual stimulation or the social stimulation of your pre-child life.

Other parents worry about leaving their newly adopted child with another caregiver or family member. This is also normal. Because your child is feeling more attached to you, he will trust this bond and figure out the transition with your help.

Child Care Considerations

You may decide to have child care provided in your home, or you may choose to use child care at your place of employment or some-where else. Wherever you decide, introduce your child to the new caregivers slowly. Have the sitter come to the house a few times, while you're still there. Or, go to the child care center and stay with your child while he plays. Consider going back to work half-days, or part-time, if you can.

Make sure you tell your child care providers whatever history you're comfortable sharing about your child. It's not necessarily important that they know that he's adopted; what's important is that they understand there has been a transition in primary caregivers and there may be some incomplete information about what you know of your child's history. You may not know how your child used to nap or how he learned to feed himself. When your child is hurt or sad, you probably respond differently than what he was accus-tomed to. A new caregiver may also provoke different reactions or responses from your child. This possibility doesn't mean that your child isn't in good hands. Keep a line of open communication going, and hopefully, any early challenges will dissipate with time.

Don't feel shy about checking in with your child care provider—multiple times daily, if necessary. Whether your child is in child care or at home with a sitter, a good provider knows to expect this communication, and she can handle both you and your child!

School Considerations

If your adopted child is school age, you will need to decide where to send him. As you visit the various school options (eg, public, parochial, charter, private), talk with school personnel so you can get a sense of their comfort level in helping an adopted child transition into the classroom. This will help inform your decision about where to send him to school. If you think your child will need special education services to address issues related to learning or behavior (see Chapter 8), please also talk with those teachers and providers.

Wherever you decide to send your child, you will have to determine grade placement. If your child has never been to school before, I suggest he enter at one grade level lower than his same-age peers. Even if he has attended school before, you might consider starting him at a lower grade level to make the transition a bit smoother. You and the school may decide that after a few months, he can move up to the next grade level.

How soon do you send your child to school? During the first few weeks at home, you will figure out how comfortable your child is with other children. Maybe he already attended school, and he's asking to start again because he "misses playing with friends." Maybe he's never seen a school, but he loves being around other children his age. Maybe he's terrified to leave the house. Taking your child's feelings into account, try introducing him to his new school slowly. Perhaps visit for an hour or two for several days, then start school half-days, and gradually increase to the full-day schedule. For the first week of school, you may want to take him to school yourself, rather than having him ride the bus.

I also recommend you talk with your child's teachers ahead of time and share the parts of his adoption story that you are comfortable sharing. He won't be the only adopted child in the school, but it is important that his teachers understand that he's experiencing a major transition. Ask his teachers to communicate with you as often as possible, and don't hesitate to reach out to them to discuss what's happening at home and how you perceive the transition is going.

Your Child's Separation Anxiety

Remember that every child experiences some level of separation anxiety—it's going to happen no matter what. But with an adopted child, his reaction to separation may be unpredictable. It's likely that he didn't have an opportunity to learn how to separate well when he was an infant. Separation is a test of trust and an understanding of whether a connection is really "there." Every child deals with separation in his own way. Eventually, he will figure it out.

I never play down that your child may experience more pronounced separation anxiety or issues than a child who is not adopted. No matter the age, a child may remember, consciously or not, the feeling of having been left.

Separation troubles can look like

- Excessive crying or irritability before a transition (eg, nap time, bedtime, going to school)
- Becoming revved up at night when a child is supposed to be quieting down
- Clinging to a primary caregiver in new situations

Managing Your Child's Anxiety

Here's what I suggest to manage your child's anxiety.

- Talk, talk, talk about what happens at bedtime, or around the school drop-off, or around the event, that's causing the problem.
- Preset upcoming events. Give your child plenty of notice before something's going to happen (eg, "I'm going to work in 10 minutes," then "I'm going to work in 5 minutes").
- Listen, listen, listen and acknowledge a child's worries and fears, even if they don't make sense to you or you've already told him that you understand.

When Parents Also Experience Separation Anxiety

It's understandable that parents have increased anxiety about leaving their child. There has already been a tremendous amount of effort put into becoming parents and a fair amount of stress because of it. Many worry that when they go back to work, or send their newly adopted child off to school, that their child won't remember them. They fear their child won't love them because he'll now attach to a sitter or teacher. If it's helpful, parents may ask that child care providers or teachers communicate with them more frequently about how their child's activities are going during the day. In the meantime, parents can ease their anxiety by taking a deep breath and by enjoying the times they *do* get to spend with their child. Children remember the *quality* time they spend with their parents.

Robin remembers...

In retrospect, I realize that I experienced my own version of separation anxiety when I first left my daughter with a babysitter a few mornings a week. I not only missed her but also didn't feel anyone else could be as attuned to what she needed and wanted. Of course, that wasn't true—she was in good hands—and I appreciated the time to work. Otherwise, she wouldn't let me out of her sight—she would follow me into the bathroom! I still feel separation pangs—the first day of preschool, the first day she bounded onto the school bus without looking back, her first sleepover, dropping her off at sleepaway camp. I know that's exactly what should happen—and I'm proud of her independence—but I still feel it. My little girl is growing up!

Time for Testing

The first month she was home, my 2-year-old was very well-behaved, almost too well-behaved, I thought, for her age. But after that month, Reilly turned into a typical 2-year-old. She started throwing tantrums and screaming at the top of her lungs when she didn't get her way. When I told her no, she would defiantly repeat the behavior I had scolded her about. One day, I found Reilly playing in the bathroom, with the toilet paper all over the floor. She was becoming her own person, and I realized that she finally felt safe with me and in our home.

— Lynn, mother of Reilly, aged 2 years

Some families confide that their "little angel," well-behaved at first, is now stubborn, throwing tantrums, or refusing to get dressed. Why is it that your once-shy child now hits, bites, or kicks his siblings or playmates? What's going on? I reassure my parents, it's all right. You are being tested, and testing is developmentally appropriate. Of course, while your child's harmful actions need to be addressed, the act of testing you as a parent is a wonderful step in the right direction in this transition process.

Why? This type of behavior is developmentally appropriate—all children test their parents. But the adoption twist is your child may have delayed this behavior until he felt comfortable and confident enough in his bond with you. What he wants is to make sure your relationship is permanent. He wants reassurance that you are always there for him. All children, of any age, want reassurance.

He may also be looking for more structure and consistency in his life. You may have taken a parenting approach where "anything goes" in your house. You felt that because your child may have been neglected and deprived, you'd let him do whatever he wants. Sometimes, disruptive behavior is a cry for structure. Orphanages and many foster homes often have rules and restrictions. Your child generally knew what to expect. When he acts out now, he may be looking for some order in his life. Make sure you stick to routines as best as you can. Get up at the same time every day. Serve meals at the same time every day. Put your child to bed at the same time, with a consistent bedtime routine, every evening.

Not all children go through this phase. And this testing often depends on age. I've seen children who are adopted at age 4 years have their "testing phase" as 7-year-olds, when they lie, steal, and hoard. Somewhere deep in his brain, in his subconscious, your child is making sure that you are there for him forever. Your job is to teach your child the appropriate way to behave and to make sure he understands that while you *don't like his behavior,* you always *love him* and will love him forever.

It is essential to establish a consistent method of discipline right from the beginning. Your child is looking for structure and needs to know what rules to follow. Your job is to be clear and consistent. If you're in a 2-parent household, this job can be difficult if one parent is the "disciplinarian" and the other parent is the "softy." Try to agree on some fundamentals of parenting. Make sure your child knows what is expected from him and what the consequences are when the rules are not followed. It's critical that your discipline technique is consistent. If you're going to allow your child to swing on the stairway gate sometimes, you're going to have to let him do it all the time. Be sure to use consistent language, and direct the language at the behavior you want to change, not the child. Instead of saying, "You're a bad boy when you pull the dog's tail," say, "Don't pull the dog's tail. That's dangerous." (See Chapter 6 for additional suggestions.)

How You Are Doing

Was it her bedtime already? Where had the day gone? I don't think I had showered that day, and I couldn't remember whether I had checked the mailbox. All I had done was make meals, feed her, clean up, play, nap, and change diapers. I couldn't remember the last time I spoke with a friend. I needed a haircut. What had happened?

—*Brooke, mother of a newly adopted 2-year-old*

Last, but not least, let's check in with you and on how you are doing. Too often, parents don't give themselves the time for the rest and recovery they need. You need to take care of yourself to be able to take care of your child.

The stress of being a parent may be intensified with the feeling that you now have what you always wanted, so you should be happy and grateful. But the reality is that it's hard to be a parent! Some adopted parents are even less likely to share their frustrations and unhappiness because they so desperately wanted to become parents. There doesn't seem to be much room to express any negative emotions about the stress of finally forming a family.

But let's be honest. Most parents are overwhelmed from time to time, no matter how they became parents. What are you doing to take care of yourself? Are you eating 3 meals a day? Are you getting enough sleep? If your child is napping, try to nap when he does, even if it's only a quick 10 minutes off your feet—don't assume you're going to get everything done when your child is asleep. You need rest too. Have you gotten back into some sort of exercise routine—whether that's yoga, going to the gym, or walking or running? Taking care of yourself physically is one way to help you have the emotional energy to take care of your family.

If you're parenting with a spouse or partner, don't forget to spend some time on your relationship. It has probably been disrupted as both of you have shifted your focus from each other and the pre-adoption process to your new family. But you can still have a "date night"—maybe with modifications! Have date night at home. Eat dessert together after your child goes to bed. Dedicate some adult time for yourselves, and make sure your child sees this. It's important that he learn how parents behave with each other in a loving manner.

Post-adoption Depression

Parenting is hard work, and it's easy to get exhausted both emotionally and physically. Parents who have adopted—who have worked so hard to build a family—may feel guilty or ashamed to feel less than happy or less than pleased all the time. That feeling can be further exacerbated if attachment is complicated. But feelings of stress or sadness are real and need to be addressed.

Yes, post-adoption depression is real, like postpartum depression, and can occur in both parents. Post-adoption depression may be more common in adults with histories of depression, is unrelated to hormones, and is generally thought of as periods of sadness, depersonalization, and not so much the fluctuation of ups and downs. (This depression contrasts with postpartum depression, which is often hormone driven and experienced as highs and lows, with many weepy periods.)

Recent research suggests that a parent who has post-adoption depression is likely to have had a bout of depression earlier in life, but a parent who hasn't experienced depression before could also experience "post-adoption blues."[1] One research study suggests that the catalyst for post-adoption depression is stress, rather than the adoption itself.[2] In addition, fathers can have post-adoption depression. In a study, fathers described this depression as anger resulting from, for instance, failing to solve problems related to the adoption, feeling let down by the professionals, lack of proper information about the child's history, and lack of support. Mothers tended to describe this depression as feelings of fatigue, lack of trust in the child, and an absence of mutual bonding.[3] *The Post-Adoption Blues: Overcoming the Unforeseen Challenges of Adoption* by Karen J. Foli, PhD, and John R. Thompson, MD, is a great resource on this topic.

If you feel that you are experiencing post-adoption blues or depression, please get the help you need. Talk with your pediatrician as well as your general practitioner. And make sure to make time for yourself—for sleep, exercise, nutritious meals, and good self-care.

Moving Forward

What's next? You and your pediatrician will determine when you bring your child back for the next visit. Depending on how things are going, she may want to see you and your child in 2 weeks or 2 months. Regardless of the interval, the frequency of visits will be greater for an adopted child, when compared with the AAP recommended well-child visits (also called *health supervision visits*). (Newborns who are domestically adopted will typically follow the AAP recommended schedule). Eventually, your pediatrician will most likely recommend annual well-child visits. This ensures that additional attention is paid to all aspects of your child's health. Remember, you don't need to wait until the next scheduled visit if any medical, developmental or behavioral concerns arise. Reach out to your pediatrician. That's why she's there!

CHAPTER 5

Health Issues and Conditions

*I*n this chapter, I discuss health conditions I often encounter in my adoption medicine practice, but please note that this list is incomplete. As I mentioned in the introduction, more families are adopting children who have already been diagnosed as having a specific medical need. For example, most children who are currently being adopted from China have a documented specific medical need. Children adopted domestically as newborns may also have well-documented, preexisting health conditions. Children adopted through foster care are likely to have medical conditions or mental health issues (or both).

If you know you are going to adopt a child with a health condition, please learn as much as you can about the condition ahead of time. Find local medical providers or therapists who specialize in the health condition, and talk with your adoption medical specialist as well. Talk with families who have had personal experience. You can also contact national organizations, such as the American Cleft Palate-Craniofacial Association, so you can find out what to expect. Don't forget that the American Academy of Pediatrics HealthyChildren.org Web site is a wonderful resource to find reliable medical information.

There's also a chance that your pediatrician might discover an unknown condition after your child's first pediatric visit. And as I've said before, it is possible that some of the medical information you have may be inaccurate or incomplete. Although unlikely, your child may have a syndrome—a set of associated medical signs and symptoms—that has not been previously described. While this possibility may sound scary and overwhelming, being prepared with what to know and being prepared for some surprises are the best approaches to move forward.

Timely and appropriate medical care will improve a child's health, as will the loving embrace of a family. You are your child's best advocate. Working with your pediatrician, you will be able to get your child the medical care she needs, now and as she gets older.

Prenatal Exposure to Substances

The American Academy of Pediatrics suggests that all adopted children be evaluated for possible exposure to drugs and alcohol in utero. Please know that pregnant women may use a wide variety of licit and illicit substances. Exposure to licit substances, such as tobacco and alcohol, and illicit substances, such as opioids, is more common among adopted children and children in foster care. Thus, it is helpful for adoptive families to understand fetal alcohol spectrum disorder and neonatal abstinence syndrome, 2 medical conditions that occur more commonly in adopted children.

Children who have had prenatal exposure to drugs or alcohol are at a higher risk for problems with development, behavior, and learning. That isn't to say that a problem will definitely develop, as I can't predict who will be affected, but since the risk is increased, it's important to understand possible difficulties. I have seen, however, and research suggests,[1] that children who have been exposed to prenatal substances do better in a safe, supportive, stimulating, and nurturing environment.

Fetal Alcohol Spectrum Disorder

Fetal alcohol spectrum disorder (FASD) includes a wide range of conditions caused by prenatal exposure to alcohol. Fetal alcohol syndrome (FAS) is the most severe form of FASD and includes facial abnormalities, growth deficits, and central nervous system involvement. Less severe forms of FASD include partial FAS, which is related to a history of alcohol exposure in utero, but not all the diagnostic features of FAS are present. Children with alcohol-related neurodevelopmental disorder do not have the facial characteristics of children with FAS nor do they have growth deficiencies, but they do have challenges with learning and behavior. Finally, prenatal alcohol exposure can cause problems with specific body organs, such as the heart and the kidneys.

Prenatal alcohol use is always considered harmful to a developing brain and body. No known level of alcohol consumption anytime during pregnancy is considered safe. Alcohol causes direct injury to the brain and changes how the brain functions. Alcohol may also cause problems with learning and behavior in the long term. It doesn't matter when or how much a birth mother drank during the pregnancy.

As I noted earlier, *all children with involvement in foster care or adoption processes, both domestic and international, should always be evaluated for possible FASD.*

Prenatal alcohol exposure in adopted children is a common concern. Even if a birth mother denies drinking during pregnancy, you don't know for sure what the birth mother did or didn't do.

> "Many adopted children have experienced prenatal exposure to alcohol and other substances. Fortunately, not all children will be negatively affected."
> — *Claire D. Coles, PhD*

Diagnosis

Diagnosing FASD is not always easy. Children with FAS will have typical facial features, growth deficiencies, and some sort of learning or behavioral problems. Growth deficiencies are apparent at birth. A newborn will be underweight, have a small head, and be shorter. However, typical facial features may not be present at birth or even within the first few years, as the features can take some time to develop.

Toddlers may have delays in motor skills and language but a high activity level. Their attention spans may be shorter than those of their peers. A toddler's frustration tolerance is low. She may have frequent tantrums and difficulty adapting to change or following directions.

At school age, specific delays in learning might become more pronounced. ADHD (attention-deficit/hyperactivity disorder) may be suspected. (See Chapter 8.) School-aged children may have a hard time learning from past experiences, understanding cause and effect, and navigating social situations.

As children mature, the condition doesn't worsen, but increased demands and expectations may exacerbate a child's issues. She may feel anxious or depressed and have low self-esteem and motivation. More-inappropriate social behavior may occur, such as lying or stealing, substance use, or inappropriate sexual behavior. Inability to read social cues may lead to problems with sustaining friendships.

Management

It's best to intervene early if your child has FASD. Providing personalized care and meeting your child's specific needs provides the best opportunity of mitigating the effects. Your child will likely need support throughout her life, and you will be her best advocate.

Some families can work with their pediatricians to help make a diagnosis. Other families use a developmental and behavioral pediatrician, a pediatric geneticist, or a pediatric neurologist. Whatever health care professional you choose, make sure that she can help you advocate for your child's needs—perhaps through your school district or your county or various local or state agencies.

Neonatal Abstinence Syndrome

Neonatal abstinence syndrome (NAS) refers to a newborn experiencing opioid withdrawal that can occur in 55% to 94% of newborns whose mothers were addicted to or treated with opioids while pregnant.[2] It may be easier to think of this condition as neonatal withdrawal rather than neonatal abstinence, as a newborn isn't able to abstain from taking an opioid.

Over the past 15 years, there has been a 400% increase in the incidence of NAS because of the rising number of pregnant mothers who either are using the opioid class of drugs, such as hydrocodone and acetaminophen (Vicodin), oxycodone (OxyContin), oxycodone and acetaminophen (Percocet), and heroin, or are on methadone or buprenorphine to break their addiction.[2] Drug use by a pregnant mother can adversely affect a developing fetus, as the drugs pass through the placental barrier. Even methadone use can cause NAS. The opioid epidemic is driving a dramatic increase in the number of children who are entering foster care. Babies made up a larger share of children going into foster care in 2014 than they did 10 years ago.[2]

As the number of mothers who use opioids has increased dramatically, so has the number of newborns placed into foster care when either the newborn or the mother tests positive for a drug. (Federal laws require hospital staff to contact child protective services.) According to the National Institute on Drug Abuse, every 25 minutes, a newborn is born with opioid withdrawal.[3]

Diagnosis

A newborn with NAS may be born preterm and have a low birth weight. A diagnosis of NAS is made by using a standardized rating system that analyzes withdrawal symptoms that occur 24 to 72 hours after birth. These symptoms include

- Tremors, hyperactive reflexes, and seizures
- Excessive or high-pitched crying, irritability, yawning, stuffy nose, sneezing, and sleep disturbances
- Poor feeding and sucking, vomiting, loose stools, dehydration, and poor weight gain
- Increased sweating, temperature instability, and fever

Treatment

In the hospital, a newborn will get an oral solution of morphine or methadone until symptoms subside, and the newborn is feeling better. The newborn may need to be cared for in the hospital for at least a week. She will be kept in a low-stimulation environment. Sometimes, babies are discharged home on medication that a pediatrician can help monitor. Once home, parents will want to maintain this same type of environment: low lights, little noise, gentle soothing, and some massage. Babies respond very well to these interventions.

Long-term Treatment and Consequences

The long-term effects of NAS are not as predictable nor as well studied as the effects of alcohol exposure. The effects may include delays in speech, cognition, and perception. There may also be behavioral consequences, such as ADHD, or a higher sensitivity to the environment (ie, sensory integration disorder; please see Chapter 8).

Cleft Lip and Palate

Many babies and toddlers who are being adopted from China are born with a cleft lip or a cleft palate (or both), a condition that happens to 1 in every 700 newborns.[4] This common defect is not usually associated with other problems.

When I first see newly adopted children from China who were born with a cleft lip, most have had their lips repaired before coming to the United States, but they may still need another operation to fix their palates. The timing of the lip repair depends on the orphanage and the availability of surgical care. It's best for your child to have lip surgery early in the first year after birth, so your child can learn to effectively suck on a bottle. Medical records might include the date of surgery, or sometimes the date of surgical correction can be estimated by using other data, such as a big jump in a child's weight.

Having a cleft lip creates a suction problem when it comes to feeding. The baby needs a special nipple as well as a skilled provider who has the time and patience to feed a baby with a cleft lip. I'm always concerned about whether a child with an unrepaired cleft lip has received adequate nutrition.

An unrepaired cleft palate increases the risks of ear infection and sinus infection. A child with a cleft palate has not typically received surgery in her native country. While cleft palates are typically repaired in the second year after birth in the United States, I've seen children who are as old as 7 to 9 years who have unrepaired cleft palates, and they have figured out how to eat without problems. They can still have their palates repaired, which will help reduce infections and help with speech production.

Treatment

I advise parents to have their children home with them 2 to 6 months before scheduling surgery. You will want your child to be bonded with you and to feel comfortable in her new environment. Many hospitals have cleft lip and palate clinics to coordinate the various physicians and specialists with expertise in cleft lip and palate: surgeons; ears, nose, and throat specialists; audiologists; speech and language therapists; dieticians; and dentists. The surgical team will coordinate the timing of future repairs. The audiological team will ensure that a child's hearing is good. Speech and language therapists will work with the child to overcome articulation challenges. Dieticians will help ensure that the child receives adequate calories for growth. A dentist will follow tooth development for appropriate alignment.

The adopted children I've worked with have tolerated their cleft lip and palate repairs extremely well. Some need to have follow-up surgery, and others may have some cosmetic plastic surgery on the lip.

Spina Bifida

Spina bifida, including spina bifida occulta, myelomeningoceles, and meningoceles, occurs when the spinal bones fail to close properly during early formation as a fetus grows inside the mother's uterus. As a result, a small sac develops, which may or may not contain nerves of the spinal cord. The nerves become trapped, and even after surgery, they become damaged. This damage affects muscles of the lower body, causing some degree of muscle weakness in the legs. A child who has spina bifida may be able to walk with a brace or walker; if not, she will need a wheelchair. Spina bifida may also affect the nerves that control the intestines and the bladder, so many children have trouble with constipation and urination. The condition occurs at about 1 in 1,000 births.[5]

Early medical records may indicate that your child had surgery shortly after birth, and now, she's doing fine. You may see photos or videos of her standing or walking. While these details seem promising, they present only a snapshot in time and are not a predictor of ability down the road.

You may receive a medical record that includes a head computed tomography scan (also known as a *CT scan*). Many children with spina bifida have hydrocephalus—an excessive amount of fluid that cushions the brain. Children with hydrocephalus require a ventriculoperitoneal shunt. This shunt drains the extra fluid from the brain and empties it into the peritoneal cavity (the fluid area in the abdomen).

Diagnosis

Diagnosis of spina bifida is most commonly made when a newborn is born. (There is an uncommon type of spina bifida, *spina bifida occulta,* that may not be recognized at birth.) Surgery is required within the first few days to close the opening in the spine.

Treatment

Spina bifida clinics exist in most major children's hospitals, so your child will receive care from multiple pediatric subspecialists. It's difficult to say how much medical intervention will be required, but you will most likely be working with a pediatric neurosurgeon, a pediatric neurologist, a pediatric gastroenterologist, a pediatric urologist, a physiatrist, and a physical therapist. Children with spina bifida often have learning challenges, so you will also need to be an advocate through your school district.

Cerebral Palsy

Impairment in the area of the brain that controls movement and muscle tone causes cerebral palsy (CP). A child with CP will have difficulty with motor control and movement, although there are many different degrees of difficulty. For some, CP is on one side of the body; for others, on both sides. Muscle tone can be very tight—called *spasticity*—or too limp—called *hypotonia*.

Cerebral palsy is caused by some brain malformation that happens, usually, during pregnancy and occasionally during delivery. Babies who are born preterm are at increased risk of developing CP.

Diagnosis

The diagnosis of cerebral palsy can be difficult to make. If you notice any delays in achieving motor milestones, please tell your pediatrician. In a baby younger than 6 months, this delay might include your baby feeling stiff or floppy, or her head may lag. When your baby is crawling, does she drag one side while pushing with the other hand and leg? Or, does she scoot on her bottom and not crawl on all fours? (Not all babies crawl, so don't panic—check it out with your pediatrician.)

If your physician suspects CP, she may obtain a CT scan or a magnetic resonance image (also known as an *MRI*) to see if there is a brain abnormality. Sometimes no brain abnormalities are noted, and you may never know why your child developed CP. Until she is 3 to 4 years of age, you may not know how severe the disability will be.

Treatment

The goal of CP treatment is to manage the symptoms to maximize a child's quality of life. Depending on the severity, some children with CP require minimal intervention, while others require intensive treatment and medical management. Treatment includes early intervention programs, for children younger than 3 years, through which children can receive physical therapy, occupational therapy, and speech and language therapy. Some children require special education classes. Older children can receive the same services through their respective school districts. Children with CP can be treated with certain medications that can help with spasticity. Many different types of adaptive equipment are available to help children walk, or they provide support with sitting upright.

Some associated problems include intellectual disability and learning challenges, seizures, hearing and vision difficulties, scoliosis, and joint problems. Not all children with CP will have all these problems, and the degree of these problems can vary. Children with CP are best served by a team of physicians and specialists, who will work closely with your family.

Hearing Loss, Ear Issues, and Ear Deformities

Hearing loss occurs for several reasons. Your child may have been born with hearing loss or may have a syndrome that includes hearing loss. Certain ear deformities, such as absence of the external ear, are associated with hearing loss. Frequent ear infections may result in hearing loss. Excessive middle-ear fluid caused by colds or allergies can cause mild hearing loss. Exposure to gunshots or other excessively loud noises can also cause inner-ear injury and hearing loss.

Please have an audiologist evaluate your child's hearing shortly after adoption to make sure that your child is hearing appropriately. For a child to understand language and produce clear speech, she needs to be able to hear well. If your child is diagnosed as having hearing loss, she will be referred to a pediatric ears, nose, and throat physician. Sometimes, ear tubes need to be inserted if the inner-ear fluid persists and doesn't drain naturally.

If your child has an ear deformity, she may need to see several pediatric subspecialists to address any hearing loss and surgical repair of the deformity.

Vision Problems

I encounter a number of vision problems in adopted children. Some of the most common issues occur in children who are either nearsighted or farsighted. Both of these conditions can be treated with corrective lenses. If your child's eyes appear misaligned or crossed, she may have strabismus, a condition in which one eye or both eyes can drift away from the nose or look crossed. For proper vision, both eyes need to work together. Sometimes, surgery is required to correct the crossing. I occasionally see a child who's been diagnosed as having strabismus but who has *pseudostrabismus*. This term describes what looks like an inward turning eye, which is hiding behind part of the nasal bridge. There is no "real" crossing. This condition can be monitored by your pediatrician and does not require ongoing follow-up by an ophthalmologist.

Lazy eye, or amblyopia, occurs when the affected eye doesn't see well or has been injured. Sometimes the diagnosis is delayed, as the physical signs can be subtle. It's important to address this condition as early as possible to ensure the best possible vision long-term. Treatments include patching the healthy eye and eye drops; both therapies help the weaker eye become stronger.

Again, please have your child's vision assessed shortly after adoption. Pediatric ophthalmologists will be able to address any specific vision concern mentioned in this chapter.

Congenital Heart Defects

Congenital heart defects are the most common type of birth defect. Heart defects can run in families, but they can also occur if a birth mother took certain medications, had diabetes, smoked cigarettes, or drank alcohol. The defects can involve various parts of the heart, including the major blood vessels. Problems can include septal defects (holes in the heart), abnormalities of heart valves, and rhythm disturbances. Sometimes the heart problem can be very serious and life-threatening, and sometimes the defect goes away over time.

While it's impossible to describe every type of defect in this book, it may help to understand defects by where they occur in the heart. Septal defects (holes in the heart) can occur in between the heart chambers, either the ventricles or the atria, or, rarely, both. Heart valves can be malformed—or stenotic—and that malformation may prohibit blood flow.

Symptoms

Children with severe heart defects will often be symptomatic. They may have shortness of breath, pale skin, swelling, trouble feeding, and trouble gaining weight. Children with milder defects may not have any symptoms at all, and the diagnosis is made only after the pediatrician performs a physical examination. Sometimes a heart defect is not discovered for several months or years after a child has been adopted.

Diagnosis

I have seen many children who were diagnosed as having a heart condition, and, after evaluation by a pediatric cardiologist and me, the condition has disappeared. Some heart conditions do resolve themselves with time. If you are considering adopting a child with a heart condition, be sure to have a pediatrician or pediatric cardiologist review any medical records. After adoption, your child should see a pediatric cardiologist, who will most likely order an electrocardiogram and a heart ultrasound (echocardiogram) to evaluate the heart's structure and function.

Treatment

Treatment of heart conditions depends on the type of heart condition. Some conditions will never require surgery, while others may require surgery or cardiac catheterization (or both). Some children will require medication to help the heart function. Children who have had open heart surgery at a young age are at increased risk of learning disabilities, so they will need to be followed closely as they go through school.

Hepatitis

Hepatitis means inflammation of the liver. This inflammation can be caused by a wide variety of toxins, drugs, and metabolic diseases, as well as an infection. At your child's first visit, your pediatrician will test for hepatitis A, hepatitis B, and hepatitis C. While it is unlikely that your child will have hepatitis, it's important to screen for this inflammation because adopted children are at increased risk because of adverse prenatal histories and some pre-adoption environmental exposures. These diseases are caused by 3 different viruses, have different modes of transmission, and can affect the liver differently.

Hepatitis A

Hepatitis A is a self-limited viral infection. Children contract hepatitis A from contact with food and water. They often don't even have symptoms, but they are contagious. A blood test can show whether your child is acutely infected or has had the infection in the past. Regardless, I recommend that all caregivers and adult family members be vaccinated. Many adults did not receive the vaccination as kids, and there have been instances in which a family member contracted hepatitis A from an internationally adopted child and died.

Hepatitis B

Your pediatrician will test for hepatitis B, which is spread via infected blood and body fluids. The disease can be chronic or acute, and in a younger child, it can develop into a chronic condition. If the test result is positive, your pediatrician should retest for confirmation. (Even if your child's first test result is negative, the test should be repeated 6 months after arrival, in case your child was infected right before the adoption, and her body hasn't had a chance to mount an immune response.) A positive test result can mean that your child was appropriately immunized, or it can mean that she had been infected at one time and is no longer infected, or she is actively infected. Hepatitis B test results require careful interpretation, and your pediatrician may decide to consult with a pediatric infectious disease specialist or a pediatric gastroenterologist (a physician with special experience in liver disease).

Signs and Symptoms

Some children who are infected with the hepatitis B virus never feel sick. Others have symptoms that might last for several weeks. Symptoms include loss of appetite; fatigue; pains in muscles, joints, or the stomach; diarrhea; and vomiting. Jaundice may also be present.

Even if a child gets over an initial bout of hepatitis B, the disease can also cause long-term (chronic) illness that leads to liver damage (cirrhosis) or liver cancer.

What You Can Do

Most children who develop hepatitis B will have normal childhoods and will reach adulthood with no serious problems. Please make sure everyone in your family, and any caregivers who spend significant time with your child, receives the hepatitis B vaccine.

Be sure to follow up with your child's specialist and follow her recommendations for ongoing monitoring. If infected, your child will need to have her blood tested several times a year.

Hepatitis C

Hepatitis C, which is a chronic condition, rarely appears in adopted children, although it is the most common of the hepatitis viruses found in children adopted from foster care and should be especially considered if a child was born to a parent who was using drugs. Hepatitis C, like hepatitis B, is contracted through blood or body fluids. It is detected in the blood during routine screening. Currently, there is no vaccine available to prevent hepatitis C. There are, however, new drugs that are being used to treat hepatitis C.

Being Your Child's Best Advocate

Caring for a child with special health care needs is often quite challenging and requires more emotional and sometimes more financial resources. Your pediatrician is your partner, and she will help you seek out any additional resources that you need. Watching a medically fragile child blossom into a thriving individual is both rewarding and inspiring.

CHAPTER 6

Attachment: The Foundation of Connections

My 2-year-old was well cared for in her orphanage in India, and she had bonded with her caregivers. When we brought Hailey home, I could see how attached she was. She mourned the loss of what she had known. One day, she had a full-blown tantrum, an exhausting episode for both of us. But I felt she was telling me: "I need to have a massive fit and let go of some of my grief." She did, and when it was over I held her. I had to fully immerse myself in her healing, and slowly she came out of her shell. And I believe because her caregivers at the Indian orphanage loved Hailey so much, she was able to love us back.

— *Cathy and Richard, parents to 2-year-old Hailey, adopted from India*

*A*ttachment is a core issue for adoptive families. Let's be honest—we have all wondered whether we could love our adopted children enough and whether they would be able to love us in return. For many parents, it's "love at first sight" and a gradual deepening of that love, as with any child. But we may silently worry how our child feels—and how we feel. There's no such thing as "instant attachment" for any parent and child. Emotional connection deepens over time, and it results from the day-to-day care that comes from being a parent and spending time with your child.

Both Robin and I understand why parents worry about attachment—we did too. However, in my practice I reassure families that in most cases all goes well over time. At every appointment, I make sure to ask parents: "How are things going? Do you have concerns about bonding and attachment?" I intentionally address these unspoken issues because some parents find it hard to articulate these feelings. Who wants to admit out loud that you wonder whether everyone loves each other? That you wonder whether your child loves you? But these concerns are normal and often crop up during the first months of being a family and may resurface later in childhood, for both you and your child.

"Attachment as an infant to a primary caregiver is one of the cornerstones of child development and paramount for the development of a lifetime of healthy relationships."
— *Christine Narad Mason, DNP, C-PNP; Susan Branco Alvarado, MAEd, LPC; and Patrick W. Mason, MD, PhD*

This chapter discusses the "dance" of attachment—how every day you and your child build the blocks of a secure and enduring relationship. I like to describe this dance as your child figuring out how to regulate his trust "barometer" as he learns that you will be there for him both physically and emotionally. Remember, this may be a very new experience for your child if he never had the chance to securely attach to a caregiver. Every child's experience is unique, and it depends, in part, on his early life experiences, his age at adoption, his personality, and your family dynamics.

Attachment is a two-way street. The parent reaches out to the child constantly with patience and understanding. However, if that feeling is one-way, you may find it difficult when there's no reciprocation from your child, especially if your efforts are rebuffed or rejected. It can be hard to be understanding and to initiate positive interactions when your child responds in a manner that's different from what you expect or desire.

Adopted children are more likely to struggle with attachment and relationships as a result of their histories, but that doesn't mean they will. There's not an easy way to say how many children might experience difficulties with attachment or who is at risk. Again, I want to prepare you for the possibilities, so you will not be surprised if things don't go the way you had hoped they would or you are faced with an attachment-related situation.

What Attachment Means

In the mid-20th century, British psychiatrist John Bowlby outlined his theory of attachment, which is still used today. He discussed the crucial role of a baby's early intimate relationship with his mother, particularly during the first 3 months after birth. (Bowlby considered the primary attachment figure to be the mother, but of course, the caregiver could be either parent, a grandparent, or a close relative.) He posited that a stable bond between caregiver and child underlies future long-term relationships. However, if this relationship was disrupted because of separation or loss, he noted that the child, as he grew up, would be susceptible to anxiety, anger, and fear.

Now I know this theory must sound scary. Does this mean that your child won't attach to you and won't be capable of having long-term, stable relationships? Absolutely not! Bowlby's theory suggests that a child may be *susceptible,* and susceptible does not mean predestined. Children are amazingly adaptable, and most adopted children I have cared for figure out how to trust and attach to their new families.

All babies, adopted or not, have a biological instinct to keep a primary caregiver close so their needs for protection, comfort, and security can be met. These needs include feeding as well as emotional needs, such as soothing feelings of fright, discomfort, or uncertainty. Through repeated interactions, a caregiver answers those needs, thus providing a baby with reassurance, protection, and calming strategies. As a result, a strongly attached child is better able to handle emotional situations and has emotional security. He will view the world as a loving place and himself as lovable.

If a caregiver is unresponsive or unavailable, a child will not have a secure attachment. He may develop behaviors to attract the attention he needs, such as crying and fussing, but he will not be able to self-soothe as well or regulate his moods. He might not view the world as a hospitable place.

Now you are your child's caregiver, providing him with the nurturance he needs. It might take time, but your consistent and sensitive presence will soothe and comfort your child.

Attachment Challenges

As I noted earlier, every adopted child will have a different experience based on who they are and their first few months and years of life. The more time your child spent in a challenging environment from birth through his early years, the more likely he may have difficulty attaching. Let's look at the key factors that can influence how attachment occurs.

Age and Attachment

How old was your child when you adopted him? If you adopted your child as a newborn or an infant younger than 6 months, he will have had fewer challenging experiences before joining your family. Older children, on the other hand, will have spent more time in prior living situations that may not have been conducive to positive attachment. They may also have more memories—conscious or unconscious—of prior living situations, and they may grieve the place and caregivers they left.

Placements and Attachment

How many prior placements (or previous living environments) has your child had? What kind of care was he in? An institution? An orphanage? Did he have different foster care families? What were those environments like? What do you know—or not know—about his care? The answers to those questions will help you figure out why attachment might be hard. Your child probably didn't have consistent responses to his needs nor a high quality of care.

If your child lived in an orphanage, he was likely taken care of by several different caregivers. It may have been difficult for him to know which caregiver to attach to or trust. In addition, high caregiver to child ratios make a difference in an orphanage—the more children per caregiver, the less attention each child gets. He may have felt more isolated and, therefore, may have developed survival behaviors to gain attention or self-soothe because he was not receiving comfort when he needed it.

If your child is adopted from foster care, your child has experienced the trauma of being separated from his biological family, most likely because of an unstable family environment, abuse, neglect, or a parent's substance use issues. Then he was placed with a foster family or may have spent time with relatives or in residential care. In these environments, he may have experienced varied consistency in caregivers. Your child was probably very confused—in his mind and his heart—as to who was responsible for his well-being.

Even newborns separated from their birth mothers may have some degree of attachment challenges. While this possibility seems unlikely, I have cared for domestically adopted newborns who, as older children, have described a sense of loss around their birth mothers. This feeling may become an issue as your child matures and understands adoption in a more nuanced way.

Remember, your child may not know how to get his basic emotional needs met. Your child needs to learn that you are physically and emotionally available and your love is unconditional. You want your child to turn to you for support above others. You need to become the preferred caregiver. Keep in mind that establishing this preference will take time.

Promoting Healthy Attachment for Your Child

The following familiar tips on attachment are worth reiterating:

- Give your child plenty of love and attention.

- Use consistent words and behaviors around love and discipline.

- Stimulate your child by exposing him to developmentally appropriate holding, conversation, reading, music, and toys.

- If needed, approach your child as if he's younger than he really is. Try bottle-feeding a toddler or rocking him as if he's a baby.

- Match the environment to your child's disposition.

Personality and Temperament and Attachment

As you learn more about your child every day, you may get a better sense of how he will react to you. You will also see how he differentiates you from other people he does not know that well. Some children have BIG personalities and aren't timid or shy. They may seek attention from everyone. Others may be stubborn and reserved and may reject you and others. Until you really get to know your child, it may be difficult to know what he needs.

Disruptive Behavior

Parents often ask me: "Why does my child act out?" You may feel as if your child is intentionally being defiant and choosing not to attach. But please don't jump to that conclusion. Instead, consider that your child's behavior may be telling you something else. His "troublesome" behavior may be caused by distress, such as hunger or fatigue. Maybe he's in pain or feels anxious about something influenced by his early childhood experiences. Many children who are adopted worry about rejection and abandonment, despite your love and reassuring words. *Will they send me back to the orphanage? Will I get moved to another foster home?*

Remember that your child is getting to know you. He has experienced lots of change fast, which can be disconcerting, and he may know to react only from a survival perspective—if he behaves poorly, he may get attention. Acting out might be the only way he has learned to react or respond. His rejecting you may be the only way he knows how to express helplessness. He may also be testing you, to see whether you're going to stick by him. He will need your comfort, reassurance, and understanding to help him calm down.

Handling a Tantrum

I know disruptive behavior is hard to tolerate. First, please take a deep breath. Then, make sure your child is safe when he is having a tantrum. He may bang his fists on you, or he may throw his body down onto the floor. Have cushions or pillows handy. Even if you think he isn't listening, remind him that you're "right here." Then try to put words to what you think he may be experiencing: "I know you're upset because you can't go outside." "You seem so sad." "It's frustrating when it's time to say goodbye when you're having fun." When children feel they are understood, you strengthen the feelings of attachment that they need.

When the tantrum subsides, think about any triggers that led up to the tantrum, so you can potentially avoid them. Talk with your child about the episode in an age-appropriate way. Remember to use language about the behavior and to not label your child. Talk about how your child was feeling during the tantrum. Ask him what was useful, for calming him down, so you can have some strategies handy for the next time.

What **Not** *to Do*

While what *not* to do may seem obvious to you, I want to mention certain adult behaviors that can lead to further trauma for a child who is struggling to attach. Most important, never ever physically hurt your child. Your child may have already experienced physical abuse before adoption. Physical harm will only push your child farther away. Even a slap on the hand can be damaging. Your child may think it's OK to hit, if he sees you do this.

Try to keep a neutral tone and volume in your voice, and avoid overreacting and yelling. I know that at times a child's behavior can be extremely provoking. We have all been frustrated to the point of tears, feeling as if we can't stand it anymore when our child won't behave as we would like. While you might experience some immediate relief, or somehow feel "more in control," when you react with physical discipline or screaming, you will most likely regret these behaviors afterward. Your child will be frightened, and you'll risk losing the trust that you're working so hard to create.

Why Your Child Acts Out

When your child acts out, remember that the way you are feeling is probably the way your child feels. (For example, if you feel angry, he feels angry. If you feel like pulling your hair out, he feels that way too.) Your child is not misbehaving for fun or because he feels like it. Something is happening emotionally for him, and it's your job, as a parent, to try to figure this emotion out. What is he upset about? How can you help him express this emotion? As hard as it seems in the moment, it's important to resort to empathy and think about your child's history.

When to Ask for Help

When you feel situations are spinning out of control or you are questioning your parenting, it's time to get support. Please don't hesitate to ask for help. Call your pediatrician and let him know that you are having a really hard time with some discipline issues. It's much better to seek help early before situations really spin out of control.

Patterns of Attachment

During the first visit, I ask new parents what might happen if they were to leave their child alone in the examination room with me. Most of the time, parents tell me their child would be scared or upset. Sometimes, parents say that they are unsure whether their child would be upset or, perhaps, that their child wouldn't mind or care if left alone with a stranger.

I also ask parents about what happens when your child falls and scrapes his knee. Does he stop and cry, or does he continue on as if nothing happened? Does he seek and respond to comfort from you? Or, does he seem self-sufficient and not seek comfort?

These different responses tell me something. They tell me how your child learned to attach. No matter what the response, I remind parents that their child is still in the process of learning to build trust in his new home. We discuss their child's pre-adoption history and how it may have influenced the current attachment behavior.

The examples that follow illustrate certain attachment patterns I watch for.

Indiscriminate Social Behavior

James is an adorable toddler with bright blue eyes and a quick grin. He was adopted last month from an orphanage overseas. When he comes into my office, he runs up to all the nurses and tugs on their pant legs. While I'm talking with his parents, he's busy playing with my shoes and trying to climb into my lap. His hands are all over my computer keyboard, and he's playing with the mouse. When I examine him, he touches my stethoscope, my hair, and sometimes my face. His parents comment how happy he is and how friendly. I wonder whether something else is going on.

Some toddlers want to be around everybody, greeting them with a smile while running away from parents. The toddler won't check back with the parent in unfamiliar situations. If the parent tries to redirect behavior, the child ignores the parent.

When a child acts as if he has no social filter, what we are seeing is what we call *indiscriminate social behavior*. The child has few to no inhibitions and no sense of personal boundaries. He is overly familiar with strangers, letting them pick him up, or hug him, or sit on their laps.

This behavior indicates to me that the child doesn't yet understand that a parent will be attuned to his specific needs. Because he has had multiple caregivers, James had to learn to get what he needed from different people, thus his pleasing "look at me" attention-seeking behavior. He never formed a deep bond with 1 or 2 people.

Managing Indiscriminate Social Behavior

Here's what you can do for a child with indiscriminate social behavior.

- Maintain structure and sense of order in your home.
- Teach your child about social boundaries.
- Work to build trusting relationships with parents first, and then extend that effort to family members.
- Introduce the concept of "strangers" in a developmentally appropriate way.

I also suggest reining in your child's world somewhat. Try to reduce stimulation from the outside. Go back to those early nesting days, when it was just you and any other primary caregiver in your home. Resort to some regressive behaviors with your child, by which I mean treating him as if he's younger than he really is. Maybe try spoon-feeding him or sitting with him in a rocking chair. Some kids won't tolerate this behavior, so you might want to role model this behavior with a doll or a stuffed animal. See whether he will copy your behavior with his own doll or stuffed animal. In addition, take a time-out from public outings, as much as possible.

Even though this type of child is generally happy and easygoing, I want the parent to realize that the child needs to work on creating a more secure attachment to the parent. It's not always obvious to parents that their child isn't as securely attached as he should be.

This type of behavior is important to address. If a child has been ignored or treated poorly when he was young, he may be overwhelmed by stressful situations. He needs to learn you are there for him, and it's OK if he needs help.

When your child hurts himself unintentionally, use language to help him know how to feel and how to respond: "Ouch! It looks like you bumped your head. Does it hurt a little or a lot? Can I put some ice on your head to help it feel better?" Let him know by your words and actions that you will soothe him (eg, that he can seek comfort from you).

Ambivalent Attachment

> *Three-year-old Julia won't climb out of her mother's lap during our first appointment. Her mom reports that Julia won't let her out of her sight. She's "attached at the hip. I can't leave the room—I have to be in her line of sight. Even when I take a shower, she sits right outside the stall and will peek in occasionally. I haven't been able to leave the house alone since she came to live with me."*

In the office, Julia won't even look at me. I understand why she's nervous—she has had a cleft lip and palate repair, so she knows to be afraid of physicians. Yet she's acting more like a 15-month-old, burying her head in her mom's shoulder and refusing to make eye contact. She seems too afraid for this situation, clinging to her mom for dear life.

Some children turn their faces away, even if I try to glimpse at them from across the room. They are very quiet and not vocal. What I notice is that the parent can't comfort the child with an offer of a snack or drink or with reassuring words. In his own way, the child can't signal "help me/save me" to his parent.

In these cases, I'm concerned about *ambivalent attachment,* which occurs when a child feels very upset when separated from a parent but isn't comforted by that parent's return. A child may act both angry and frustrated and then abruptly become clingy and dependent.

On the one hand, a parent may think his child is very attached to him, because the child is so clingy. But, on the other hand, this death grip comes from a place of fear. When the parent leaves, the child experiences strong separation anxiety. He doesn't understand object permanence yet—that your parent is still there, just in a different room, and not leaving you.

Managing Ambivalent Attachment Behavior

Here's what you can do for a child with ambivalent attachment.

- Try some of the suggestions for a child with indiscriminate social behavior provided earlier in this chapter.

- Give your child plenty of space when he needs it. Encourage—but don't push—your child to explore on his own.

- Try some intentional separation trials. For example, when you are at home with your child, try to distract him in play. Tell him that you are going to step away into another room for a minute, and then you will be "right back." When you leave, he may scream or try to chase after you. Try to disappear out of his sight for a few minutes. When you return, exclaim: "I'm back!" Do this multiple times every day, and try to stay out of sight for longer and longer periods of time (of course, while ensuring his safety at all times). This separation might sound a bit extreme, but your child will learn to trust you. When you go away, you come back.

Disorganized Attachment

> *Eight-year-old Patrick is in my office with his adoptive mother, who fostered him for the past year. Before that, he had been in and out of 6 foster homes, beginning when he was 9 months of age. During his early infancy, he was severely neglected. He was fed inconsistently and received very little nurturing and stimulation. After he was separated from his mother, he spent some time with a relative who wasn't prepared to handle an infant with special emotional needs. He was placed in foster care within a few months. His behaviors have always been challenging. He struggles with outbursts and meltdowns. He is often hard to console and doesn't know how to ask for help. School is also a problem. In addition to the behavioral concerns he has, he requires additional academic support.*

Like children adopted internationally, children adopted from foster care may struggle to form meaningful relationships with adults during early childhood, not because they don't want to but because their home environments were unstable.

Patrick's mother is concerned that he hasn't bonded with her. When I consider Patrick's background, I remind her that he has experienced chronic instability throughout his short life. His challenging behaviors may result from how unpredictable his life has been. He may be cautious because he is afraid of being wrong. He may have been scolded repeatedly for making mistakes; perhaps he was physically abused.

He is also still learning what "normal" family expectations are. What are the rules? How should he behave? What are the consequences for misbehaving?

Because Patrick has experienced so many different care situations, he may be confused about many things. If he's able to talk about his early experiences, his parents should acknowledge his feelings and talk about those experiences now and as he gets older. It would also be helpful for him to process his experiences with a therapist who understands the complications.

Children coming from foster care may feel particularly adrift. How do they keep in touch with biological parents and siblings? If they have had to move, how do they keep connections with teachers and other adults (such as sports coaches, religious figures, and neighbors) who have played an important role in their lives? It may be very difficult for children to create lasting bonds. There are no easy answers; your child needs to learn that he can create a lasting bond with you.

Managing Disorganized Attachment Behavior

Here's what you can do for a child with disorganized attachment.

- Take cues from your child—watch for what feels safe.

- Slowly work on affection and eye contact.

- Offer language cues to describe feeling states.

- Instill humor and playfulness during your daily interactions.

- Celebrate successes such as helping out around the house, demonstrating an understanding of family rules, using appropriate language, and positive interactions with peers.

Attachment Issues in Later Years

> *Annabelle, who joined her family as a newborn, is in my office for her 13-year-old well-child visit. She is medically well, but her mom reports that Annabelle has been crying a lot, not only upset about the death of her grandmother but also devastated that her first boyfriend has broken up with her. Annabelle's mom wonders whether the cause is the teen years or something else that might be causing Annabelle's extreme distress.*

I notice that some teens, adopted at a very young age, tussle with attachment issues during adolescence. This is the time they begin to question their identities, who they are, and where they came from.

Attachment Issues During Adolescence

Here's what you can do for an adolescent struggling with attachment issues.

- Remember that the teen years are already fraught with many ups and downs!
- Talk with your pediatrician about finding a social skills group or community support group for your adolescent.
- If opting for a therapist, be certain that the therapist is sensitive to issues about adoption.

It may be difficult to sort out whether your adolescent is experiencing an attachment issue, is struggling with impulsivity, or is just being a tween or teenager. There is some evidence that when adopted children who struggle with attachment become adolescents, they may prefer adults as friends and may have more difficulties with peer relationships.

Peer relationships are already emotionally fraught, and those feelings might be intensified. Adopted teens may also struggle with relationships. For example, Annabelle's mom thought Annabelle was quite clingy with her first boyfriend. When he broke up with her 6 weeks later, she wouldn't stop crying.

Any loss in family may be magnified, whether it's the loss of a pet, the death of a grandparent, or a divorce. Instead of a reaction being on the "Wow" level, the reaction is more an extreme "WHOA!"

Your Attachment Anxiety

All parents worry, to some degree, about when and how attachment will happen. Some parents feel an immediate connection to their child, while others feel it takes longer for their bond to deepen. Certainly, if your child's behavior is rejecting or off-putting, attachment can be more challenging, even if you emotionally and intellectually understand why your child is acting that way. When attachment isn't going well, it's hard to admit that you feel overwhelmed or frustrated. As I mentioned earlier, attachment is a two-way, not a one-way, street. So what do you do when you feel as if you are being rejected?

It's important to try to respond not to the surface behavior but rather to what your child is trying to communicate. As you come to know your child better, consider what feelings are underlying the troublesome behavior. Those feelings might very well be tied to attachment. It might be difficult for your child to accept and express his dependence on you when he's used to depending on himself. It might be hard for him to express affection when his attempts before had been rebuffed. Try to keep in mind that he is trying to learn how to express himself, and when in a stressful situation, it's easier to revert to earlier learned behaviors. He needs to learn new ways of being, new ways to soothe himself, and new ways to ask for help.

Try to find a supportive community of adoptive parents or an adoption therapist who you can talk with. (Please see the Finding a Good Adoption Therapist section in Chapter 7.)

Please give yourself a break. Parenting is really hard work, and just when you think you've figured it out, your child has a major developmental burst that changes the game.

You might also want to reflect on your attachment style and what feelings are being stirred up in you if your child is having attachment issues. It's OK to admit that you were expecting an easier time of it. Most parents feel that way.

Also, consider how you were parented, whether you are a first-time parent or not. How do you feel about your attachment? How secure do you feel in your relationships? How do you handle your feelings without projecting them onto your child?

Adding a new person to a family shifts the balance of preexisting relationships. A new child brings a new personality to the table. There's a new dynamic to figure out. If you already have children, how do you handle the change in the family equilibrium? It's challenging to divide your time when you want everyone to feel loved, and each child's needs are different. Try to model healthy attachment with all family members, recognizing that preexisting relationships will require extra attention, particularly if any of those relationships includes a previously adopted child. That child may feel really insecure when a newly adopted child joins the family. Provide lots of reassurance with language—"We are a family forever"—and spend quality time with him.

Reactive Attachment Disorder

While most adopted children will develop healthy attachments with their parents, some will struggle with what is known as *reactive attachment disorder* (RAD). Reactive attachment disorder is an unusual condition in which a child rarely or minimally turns preferentially to an attachment figure for comfort, support, protection, and nurturing. Children with RAD show limited interest in interacting with caregivers. They seldom feel the need to check in with adults. Children with RAD have histories of being socially neglected or were raised in environments that had limited opportunities to form selective attachments. Now this sounds like the history of many adopted children—but we know that most adopted children *don't* develop RAD.

Reactive attachment disorder might occur if your child had insufficient care before the age of 5 years and now acts in the following manner and has had symptoms for more than a year. (The American Psychiatric Association now includes RAD as part of the trauma and stressor-related disorders category in its *Diagnostic and Statistical Manual of Mental Disorders,* the authoritative and official guide to the diagnosis of mental disorders. The fifth update was published in 2013.)

- Your child has a consistent pattern of not seeking or responding to comfort from an adult caregiver.
- Your child doesn't respond socially or emotionally to others, isn't very positive, or can be irritable, sad, or fearful with an adult caregiver, even in a nonthreatening interaction.

If your child has had these symptoms for more than a year, you may want to consider having him evaluated for RAD. However, please don't jump to any conclusions because your child's behavior matches some Internet checklist. Reactive attachment disorder should be diagnosed by a trained mental health professional, as there isn't a standard validated screening tool.

If you choose to have your child evaluated, please keep in mind that this diagnosis may be overused or not get to the heart of what your child is experiencing. For example, toxic stress or post-traumatic stress disorder (see Chapter 7) might be an underlying issue, or your child may have undiagnosed depression or anxiety. Some symptoms—such as social difficulties—overlap with behavior seen in children with autism spectrum disorder. What's important—as you seek help—is to consider the overlap with other diagnoses and not jump to the conclusion that your child has RAD.

Please keep in mind that no medication can treat RAD. However, your pediatrician or psychiatrist may recommend a medication to treat a disorder, such as depression, that can be confused for RAD. There are also a variety of evidenced-based, therapeutic models available for approaching attachment problems as well as RAD. Key components include working with a trained mental health professional to help you create a stable caregiving environment for your child, and they include giving you the tools to help him attach. Through therapy, you will learn how to create positive interactions with your child in an appropriate way for him. A therapist will also screen for and help treat any coexisting disorders such as anxiety and post-traumatic stress disorder.

You may also read about controversial therapies, such as "holding" and "coercive strategies," that are not research based. If a therapeutic technique doesn't sound right to you, or you read about "guaranteed improvement," ask your pediatrician about these approaches before trying them.

The Connection Strengthens Over Time

Be patient. Attachment takes time. It's like learning to dance with someone—at first you might step on each other's toes but then, as you become more comfortable with each another, you can anticipate your child's "next steps" and can move more gracefully, together. The parent-child connection gets stronger over time and will gain depth, as your child matures. As you experience some of the greatest joy and love in your life, you will forget much of your early angst around your initial bond. In the meantime, create an environment of safety and trust for your child. Focus on enjoying meaningful moments, and feel your connection deepen.

CHAPTER 7

Your Child's Emotional Health: What to Watch for and When to Worry

A nurse found 3-year-old Jacob hiding under a chair in an AIDS clinic in Ethiopia. He had been abandoned, and he was very ill, with broken ribs, a collapsed lung, and sepsis. After surgery, he was nursed back to health and transferred to an orphanage while he waited for his adoption to be finalized.

His behavior indicated that he had lived on the streets at some point, but no one knew exactly what happened. When Susan, his adoptive mother, visited him in the orphanage, she recalled that he once awoke from a nap with his eyes wide open but wasn't fully awake. Even though he had met Susan several times, he couldn't register who she was. Instead, he crawled back into his cot and stared at the wall.

Those trancelike states, caused by post-traumatic stress disorder, continued when Susan brought him home. "He'd go into a catatonic state, drooling, eyes rolled back in his head," she said. "I'd hold him and rock him—he never fought me. Then after 3 hours of not responding—click—the episode would end, and he would run off and play. Slowly, slowly, he'd be in these states for shorter periods to the point now when they rarely occur." She describes Jacob, now 5 years of age, as a loving kid, who is funny, athletic, and loves going to school.

> — *Susan, adopted Jacob at age 4 years from Ethiopia*

*A*s difficult as it is to consider, I encourage families I work with to understand how toxic stress and early childhood trauma may have affected their child's emotional health. The American Academy of Pediatrics advises pediatricians to consider that all children adopted or in foster care may have experienced some sort of trauma. Children adopted domestically, internationally, and from foster care have all encountered something stressful in their backgrounds that you may or may not know about. As a parent, I know it's easier *not* to think about your child being hurt or scared and helpless, but by considering that possibility you can better help her heal.

It is never a pediatrician's intent to be dire or discouraging. Children are doing the best they can, and I am amazed, again and again, by the incredible resilience I see in children every day. Most of the children I work with make great progress, and I'm in awe.

"Having at least 1 adult who is devoted to and loves a child unconditionally, who is prepared to accept and value that child for a long time, is key to helping a child overcome the stress and trauma of abuse and neglect."
(Pediatrics. *2000;106[5]:1145–1150*)

When children transition to a stable family environment, they have the best opportunity to thrive. Experts agree that adoption is overwhelmingly positive for children. Parents give so much to their child with better caregiving, stability, consistency, and structure. Your child has better nutrition, medication, stimulation, attention, and nurturing. You are there for your child, showering her with love, understanding, and affection.

Yet, if your child's reaction to some event seems out of the ordinary or new behavior patterns crop up that cause you to question what is going on, please consider the influence of your child's pre-adoption life. Events in early childhood may have been extremely stressful, and your child may be experiencing post-traumatic stress disorder. By understanding these reactions or behaviors, you can best help your child recover from stressful events in her past. Of course, her behavior could be part of a typical developmental stage. Many kids throw tantrums, display defiance, or freeze up when situations are challenging. But always keep in the back of your mind that your child's pre-adoption history could be contributing to some piece of her behavioral puzzle. If extra support is needed, you can find appropriate treatment and care.

If your child is experiencing emotional difficulties, take your child to your pediatrician. Your pediatrician will take a thorough history, which includes a family history. If your child is adopted from foster care, or is adopted domestically as a newborn, you may have some information about family mental health issues. It's important to share this information. Mental health issues run in families, and your pediatrician will want to know this history in case your child develops difficulties. Even if you don't have access to your child's family history, I recommend that your pediatrician screen for mental disorders at all medical visits, particularly at well-child visits (also called *health supervision visits*). Pediatricians have access to a variety of screening tools to assess for depression, anxiety, and other mental health conditions. Don't hesitate to ask your pediatrician to screen for these things. Even if the screening test results are negative, your pediatrician may still suggest a referral to a mental health professional.

Finding a Good Adoption Therapist

If you decide your family or your child needs to meet with a therapist, try to find a therapist who is "adoption-competent." The therapist needs to understand the issues of grief and loss your child may be grappling with plus understand the dynamics of the adoption constellation, which includes your child's birth family, your family, and your community. The therapist must be sensitive to your child's history and your family's history. Finally, she should consider the breadth of issues that may be influencing any emotional or behavioral difficulties.

Ask your pediatrician or adoption agency to recommend a therapist with experience in treating adopted children. Local adoption support groups may be able to provide references. In addition, many colleges and universities have psychology or social work programs through which you may be able to find some expertise.

There could be many reasons you would seek out a therapist; if you do, please make sure the therapist you select has experience working with adoptive families and is familiar with adoption-related issues.

Types of Stress

Everyone experiences stress, of course, and learning to deal with stress is part of life. But stress can be harder to tolerate for children who have come from adverse situations. Not every child exposed to stress will develop trauma symptoms. But certain behaviors may be linked to experiencing what is called *toxic stress*. Clinicians categorize stress into 3 levels of intensity—*positive, tolerable,* and *toxic*—to describe how one's body reacts.

Positive Stress

Positive stress is normal day-to-day stress, when your body experiences brief increases in heart rate and mild elevations in hormone levels. Your child may experience short-lived positive stress when she first meets a new sitter, when she attends her first day of preschool or child care, or when your pediatrician has to give her an injection (a shot). Positive stress is developmentally appropriate. This type of stress helps a child grow and develop appropriate coping mechanisms.

Tolerable Stress

We all experience tolerable stress from time to time. *Tolerable stress* occurs when the body's alert systems are activated to a higher degree. These experiences include more-stressful situations such as the loss of a loved one, a fire, or a frightening injury. An existing relationship with a loving adult is what makes this stress tolerable. The adult helps the child relax and allows her brain to recover from what could otherwise be damaging effects. Caring adults are nurturing and use language to help a child understand her feelings. "This is so sad for us, to say goodbye Grandpa." "I know you must have been very scared when you had to go to the emergency department after you fell off your bike and broke your arm." In addition to experiencing words of empathy, children need to know that their parents are there for them. A parent, simply sitting in the same room without talking, can comfort a child who has experienced a traumatic event.

Toxic Stress

Toxic stress involves adversity that is strong, frequent, or prolonged (or any combination thereof) and is not buffered by adequate adult support. Children who are subjected to physical, sexual, or emotional abuse; chronic neglect; exposure to violence; or the burdens of family economic hardship experience toxic stress. Some children who have lived in an orphanage or have moved from foster home to foster home have experienced toxic stress. These children may feel that adults are not to be relied on or trusted. To them, the world may seem like a dangerous place.

Age at adoption also affects the likelihood of experiencing toxic stress. The younger she is when you adopted her, the less time she had in a potentially negative, stressful environment. The longer she experienced stressful circumstances, the more effect toxic stress may have had on her.

Even if a child is adopted as a newborn, she still may have been exposed to stress. We know that fetuses respond to maternal stress, and this exposure can have long-lasting effects. A birth mother may have experienced stress during her pregnancy. During this time, she may have experienced domestic violence, may have been unable to access proper nutrition, may have had a mental health condition, or may have been unable to get the care she needed. Even the decision-making process around the adoption placement could have created enormous stress in her life.

Neurobiology of Stress

We all know how our bodies feel when we are stressed. Some researchers believe that when an infant or a young child experiences severe stress, it's possible that her body's reaction can change or "disrupt" brain connections.

Stress causes physical and emotional changes in the body, most commonly known as the "fight or flight or freeze" response. When stressful events repeat or are continual, a child gets used to being ready to run, fight back, or freeze at a moment's notice. So what may look like a bad behavior to you—for example, tantrums, anger, or inattentiveness—may be your child's way of being ready to fight to stay safe. Your child may react with a flight response and run from you; or, your child might freeze, space out, or not react, even to the point of being close to catatonic. Fleeing and freezing can be as disconcerting to a parent as a child who fights back.

When a child perceives serious threats, her body and brain automatically go into a toxic stress response. Her brain learns to protect her body in scary situations. But that learned behavior might be unnecessary once the child is placed with a loving family or within a structured, healthy school setting, and trust has been established. Consider, for example, if your child has trouble falling asleep at night or has frequent nighttime awakenings. These behaviors make sense if she slept in a scary environment—had a violent parent, for

Ways to Identify Trauma

Bodily Responses

Traumatic influence on the brain can result in changes in bodily functions. (Please note, though, that having any of these bodily challenges does not necessarily mean this challenge is a response to trauma.)

Sleep

- Difficulty falling asleep
- Difficulty staying asleep
- Nightmares

Disordered Eating

- Not knowing when one is full and difficulty in knowing satiety
- Food hoarding
- Loss of appetite

Toileting

- Constipation
- Impacted stool or encopresis (Child resists having bowel movements.)
- Bed-wetting
- Regression of toileting skills

Behavioral Responses

Trauma-induced behaviors may be adaptive and protective when a child is threatened. These responses were appropriate when the child was in a harmful situation but may not be useful now when she is in a safe place. An example is Jacob from the start of this chapter who would dissociate as a response to stress.

Adapted from American Academy of Pediatrics, Dave Thomas Foundation for Adoption. *Helping Foster and Adoptive Families Cope With Trauma.* Elk Grove Village, IL: American Academy of Pediatrics; 2015.

example, or one who came home drunk at night. These behaviors also make sense if the environment wasn't scary. Imagine being a young child who is alone, frightened in her room at night, and without any comfort. That child may also perceive bedtime as a stressful situation. The child's brain and body are trying to keep

Response to Trauma: Behaviors

Category	Most Common With	Response	Misidentified As and/or Occurs With
Dissociation	• Girls • Young children • Trauma or pain, either of which is ongoing • Inability to defend oneself	• Detachment • Numbing • Compliance • Fantasy	• Depression • ADHD or inattentiveness • Developmental delay
Arousal	• Boys • Older children • Witnesses to violence • Inability to fight or flee	• Hypervigilance • Aggression • Anxiety • Exaggerated response	• ADHD • ODD • Conduct disorder • Bipolar disorder • Anger management difficulties

Abbreviations: ADHD, attention-deficit/hyperactivity disorder; ODD, oppositional defiant disorder.

Adapted from American Academy of Pediatrics, Dave Thomas Foundation for Adoption. *Helping Foster and Adoptive Families Cope With Trauma.* Elk Grove Village, IL: American Academy of Pediatrics; 2015.

her safe. Now that she's in a safe situation, she has to unlearn that behavior. And unlearning is difficult.

If you notice your child has sleep problems, excessive or unexplained anger episodes, aggressive behaviors, anxiety, depression, or difficulties in sustaining attention, please recognize and consider the link to possible earlier stressful life experiences and talk with your pediatrician.

Post-traumatic Stress Disorder

As a pediatrician, I would love to figure out why most kids who have been adopted don't have some form of post-traumatic stress disorder (PTSD). Despite enduring stressful conditions, most of the children that I've worked with—and children my colleagues have worked with—do not show traumatic behavioral responses.

The resilience of children is remarkable. Adopted children have all experienced some degree of abandonment or trauma. Some have been abandoned, others have bounced from foster home to foster home, and many have lived in an orphanage where they didn't get their needs met in a timely manner. Even children who are adopted as newborns probably experienced some significant fetal stress because their birth mothers' circumstances may have been less than ideal. It amazes me how children not only survive but thrive.

However, I do work with children who exhibit PTSD-related behavior at various times. The American Academy of Pediatrics reports that rates of clinical PTSD as high as 25% have been found among children from foster care.[1] Post-traumatic stress disorder can also affect children who have lived in orphanages. Sometimes it shows up when a child first gets home, as it did with Jacob from the beginning of this chapter; other times PTSD-related behavior shows up when a child gets older. I've seen adopted children struggle with the first separation after adoption. If a child has been home with her adoptive parent for several years and then transitions to kindergarten, there will frequently be several weeks of intense separation difficulties. This reaction is stronger than what we typically expect from a child.

Post-traumatic stress disorder can also show up around medical procedures. I know older adopted children who freak out when they need their seventh grade vaccines. Now, lots of children don't like needles and get upset when they get shots or blood drawn, but when a child's reaction is extreme, it tells us something. It tells us that the child's brain is remembering something scary and traumatic from her past. It may be related to the pain of the needle, it may be related to the smell of an alcohol wipe, or it may be related to being restrained. One child told me: "It's like my brain knows that something happened to me a long time ago."

Post-traumatic Stress Disorder Symptoms

Post-traumatic stress disorder is defined as all the following signs:

- A tendency to persistently reexperience a traumatic event through intrusive thoughts, feelings, dreams, and flashbacks
- Avoidance of stimuli associated with the event
- Negative alterations in cognitions and mood
- Alterations in arousal and reactivity

If your child experiences 2 or more of the following symptoms when reminded of a traumatic experience, she may be experiencing PTSD. According to the *Diagnostic and Statistical Manual of Mental Disorders,* 5th Edition,[2] the symptoms include

- Insomnia
- Irritability or angry outbursts
- Poor concentration
- Memory impairment
- Startles easily
- Feeling of detachment or numbness

- Almost always seems to be watching out for danger (hypervigilance)
- Persistent emotions of fear, horror, anger, guilt, or shame

Post-traumatic Stress Disorder and Adoption

The challenge with PTSD and adoption is that many children *can't* recall the trauma because it occurred when they were very young, before they were able to talk, or they've blocked it from their memories. They relive the traumatic events through feeling, without even knowing it. In addition, the traumatic events may be nuanced. They may not be what we typically think of, when we think of PTSD that adults or soldiers experience, which is a reaction to definable, horrible events. Another confusing point is that not all children experience the world in the same way, and what's traumatic to one child may not be traumatic to another.

Whenever a parent describes a new onset of behavioral challenges, new problems with friends or at school, or new behavioral issues at home or school, I start to wonder what has happened with this child in the past. I ask parents about known past traumatic events, such as physical abuse. I also ask parents to consider things they may not have thought about: "How long did your child live on the streets, begging for food? Who was with your child in the hospital, when she had surgery? Was she by herself? What do you know about the transitions between each foster home? What do you know about each foster home placement?"

It can be very difficult to know what might trigger a traumatic response from your child. The trigger could be something as simple as a change in routine, or the traumatic response might occur when something unanticipated happens. Some children get terrified when a fire truck or police car drives by with the alarm ringing. Going to school might make a child anxious, and anxiety might trigger a traumatic memory.

Triggers can be related to sensations, sounds, smells, and feelings; even places and a certain tone of voice can act as triggers. If a person feels emotionally that something scary is happening again, some detail triggers a reaction that is more than expected. Triggers are hard to identify, and children will try to avoid them. Try to keep track of what sorts of triggers startle your child. What happened and when? How did your child react? For how long?

Remember that something little can set off a strong response. Your child is reacting to a threat you can't see or some reminder of her loss. When more-obvious losses occur—such as the loss of a pet and the death of a grandparent—your child may be more devastated than you would expect. If your child had experienced some bodily harm, she may be excessively inquisitive about injuries or overly worried for a friend going to the hospital for a simple surgery.

I have known adopted children who react strongly when a second child joins the household. The child not only can display regressive behaviors (which is typical for many children) but also can experience severe separation anxiety that manifests with meltdowns, hitting, and screaming, which won't be typical behaviors for that child. It is possible that the child is reexperiencing an initial traumatic event of neglect or abandonment.

Helping Your Child Heal

You immediately help your child by giving her a supportive, responsive relationship. You are giving her security and stability. You are teaching her that adults can be trusted and responsive. It takes time, patience, and practice for a child's brain and body to learn better ways to respond.

Your child has limited coping skills to deal with her feelings of rejection or deprivation. Keep in mind that her reaction—what psychologists would call a *dysregulated response*—may be generated by fear. It's likely your child isn't acting willfully oppositional; instead, she may feel paralyzed by overwhelming anxiety.

Consequently, your job as a parent may be more demanding. When your child is upset, she may be very difficult to calm down, hard to handle, and unable to manage her feelings. She doesn't know how to regulate this response herself. She may have learned poor coping skills. It is challenging to parent a traumatized child, and I understand if you become frustrated, angry, or exhausted. These behaviors are difficult to tolerate. But the more you can respond to your child in a calm and consistent matter, the better chance your child will unlearn her reactive behavior.

A Positive Parenting Approach

A positive parenting approach works best. I encourage you to

- Understand that any transition, no matter how insignificant, may be challenging for your child.
- Notice and look for triggers—what makes your child anxious?
- Establish routines to help your child know what to expect.
- Give your child a sense of control by offering simple choices and respecting her decisions.
- Try to stay calm and caring. Reacting may worsen an outburst.
- Try to stay responsive and available, even when your child pushes you away.
- Never use physical discipline. Doing so will especially panic a child who has experienced physical abuse.
- Set boundaries and limits with consistency and patience.
- Allow her to feel the way she feels, but teach her how to express in words what she feels and how best to handle those feelings. Then support and praise her for calming down and sharing how she feels. If she can't use words, help her with pictures or name the feelings for her.

- Let her know that her behaviors are telling her something about the past, even if that's hard to understand.
- Answer her questions in a developmentally appropriate way, so she can understand the changes and events in her life.
- Be patient. I know that's hard, but your child needs to learn to trust you.
- Show love and affection.
- Ask for help when you need it!

These suggestions are adapted from American Academy of Pediatrics, Dave Thomas Foundation for Adoption. *Helping Foster and Adoptive Families Cope With Trauma.* Elk Grove Village, IL: American Academy of Pediatrics; 2015.

When and How to Talk With Teachers and Caregivers About Your Child's Experiences

- Let teachers and caregivers know that when your child acts out, there may be more to the story than what's apparent.
- Remind them that this might be an automatic behavior.
- Offer them some suggestions as to how to respond to your child.
- Encourage them to be calmer and more patient. Escalation doesn't work. If they raise their voices or get angry with your child, your child will get even more upset and scared, which may reinforce her maladaptive behavior.
- Ask them to communicate with you frequently, so you know what to expect at home. You can do the same—if your child has a tough night, or doesn't get a good night's sleep, let her teachers and caregivers know. You don't want your child labeled as the "problem child" when her behavior is rooted in fear or anxiety.

Of course, this approach is easier said than done when you've been dealing with challenging behaviors. It's important to think about how you feel and react when you are upset and stressed. What can you do to mediate your reaction? Count to 10? Walk out of the room and come back? Ask for help if you feel overwhelmed. Remember that the way your child is making you feel is probably the way your child feels herself.

Therapies That Work

If you need help, make sure you reach out to a qualified therapist who has experience in adoption issues. Ideally, the therapist will be trained in evidence-based therapies and treatments. However, you may not have access to a therapist with this experience. In that case, it's important to find someone who understands the impact of early childhood adversities. Trauma-focused psychotherapy can help children and families with many behavioral symptoms. It's always better to get help sooner rather than later to support your family and child. Treatment of a child's emotional and behavioral problems related to her past trauma can make a difference in the short and long terms.

Consider using one of these evidence-based treatments that have been proven to work.

For children up to 5 years of age

- PCIT (Parent-Child Interaction Therapy): This therapy works to improve the quality of the parent-child relationship and any changing parent-child interaction patterns.
- CPP (Child-Parent Psychotherapy): A child and caregiver see a therapist together to see how the child's trauma affects the caregiver-child relationship and the child's development.

For older children

- TF-CBT (Trauma-Focused Cognitive Behavioral Therapy): Parents and their child work together to learn new skills to deal with symptoms of PTSD, fear, anxiety, depression, or traumatic grief.

- CBITS (Cognitive Behavioral Intervention for Trauma in Schools): This intervention is for fifth graders through high schoolers. It is a school-based program to reduce symptoms of PTSD, depression, and behavioral problems and to help with school behaviors.

For both older children and younger children

- ARC (attachment, self-regulation, and competency): This therapeutic framework targets these 3 core areas to reduce a child's PTSD and general mental health symptoms as well as increase adaptive and social skills.

These suggestions are adapted from American Academy of Pediatrics, David Thomas Foundation for Adoption. *Helping Foster and Adoptive Families Cope With Trauma.* Elk Grove Village, IL: American Academy of Pediatrics; 2015.

As Your Child Gets Older

As your child gets older, it's important to watch for anxiety, depression, and low self-esteem, as adopted children are at increased risk for these mental health issues. Children reprocess experiences at different developmental stages and ages. They may revisit feelings when they understand adoption differently or when they enter a new developmental phase, such as adolescence or young adulthood.

Parents should be concerned anytime there are major, or sometimes even subtle, changes in

- Eating
- Sleeping
- Peer relationships

- School performance
- General affect (Does your child seem increasingly sad? Does she seem more anxious?)

If you notice changes, make sure you

- Check in with teachers at school to see how your child is functioning academically and socially. Have grades suddenly dropped? Is your child having a difficult time socially at school?
- Call your pediatrician.

Suicide

Suicide is a difficult topic to discuss, but adoptive parents need to know that research shows adopted adolescents are at a higher risk of a suicide attempt than their adolescent peers are. Several studies have found that "the odds of a reported suicide attempt were about **4 times greater in adopted teens** compared with non-adopted teens."[3] An earlier study by Slap et al[4] showed that "the association persists after adjusting for depression and aggression and is not explained by impulsivity as measured by a self-reported tendency to make decisions quickly."

As Slap et al explain, most adopted adolescents don't attempt suicide. Slap et al observe that "high family connectedness decreases the likelihood of suicide attempts regardless of adoptive status and represents a protective factor for all adolescents."

However, parents need to be attuned to how their teen is feeling, especially since many teens are so good at hiding their feelings. Adopted teens have described themselves as "feeling lost or disconnected" without understanding why. This feeling may, or may not, be related to the adoption. For those who are aware of their feelings of loss and sadness regarding the adoption, they may feel "ungrateful" talking with you, because you "don't get it," or they may be processing some guilt they have about loving you and being angry at their biological parent (or parents). Becoming a young adult is complicated enough, and then the adoption piece is added on. It's often too much for a young person to process, thus the overwhelming feelings and feelings of low self-worth.

If your child attempts suicide, or you suspect your child is thinking about suicide, you must get her to your pediatrician or mental health professional immediately. Don't brush off what may seem like a teenager being "dramatic." She may have undiagnosed depression or anxiety, which can be effectively treated with medication and therapy. Mental health issues may run in your child's biological family, and, while this history may be unknown, it's important for you and your child to consider. You may feel as if you're opening a can of worms, but in the long term, doing so will be helpful for your child to understand part of who she is.

Moving Forward With Love

As your child grows up, you will always wonder and worry about her mental health. Worrying is part of being a parent. The best chance for any child to develop emotional well-being is to live in an environment of consistency, nurturing, and love. Whenever possible, helping your child develop meaningful relationships, with sustained connections, with yourself and others will provide the greatest possibility of an emotionally healthy life.

CHAPTER 8

Learning and Attention Challenges

Ella's preschool teacher told me that Ella couldn't sit still during circle time, that she didn't seem to understand how to share with her friends, and that she wasn't following instructions. Her teacher wondered whether she had ADHD (attention-deficit/hyperactivity disorder) or was having trouble learning. I thought that Ella was just acting like a typical preschooler— she is very social and has a lively personality. But in the back of my mind I wondered whether she had a learning disorder, because my older son had been diagnosed as having dyslexia. I brought Ella to the pediatrician so we could talk about what was going on.

— Gina, mom to Ella, adopted domestically
as a newborn, now 4 years of age

*C*hildren adopted internationally, domestically, or from foster care are at increased risk for learning challenges as well as attention challenges. If your child is adopted internationally, he will also be more likely to experience language delays. If your child was in an orphanage, he may have language delays because he never acquired appropriate native language, often because there was limited adult interaction. If your child was in foster care, he may have delays caused by inconsistent care or education. If your child has language delays, he will also be at increased risk for language-based learning difficulties. Various learning differences may emerge as your child learns to read, write, or master math concepts. I can't predict who will catch up or who will have ongoing needs. But knowing what to watch for means you can help your child sooner rather than later, if you think your child is starting to struggle.

Watching a child learn is an amazing process. And language acquisition is especially fun. Robin and I loved watching our children progress from cooing and babbling to understanding what we said and then talking to us. (It's less fun when your children "talk back," particularly in the tween and teen years!) In our cases, our children also had to learn English, as they had heard only Chinese for their respective first years after birth. We were stunned at how quickly they understood what we said and then how, like sponges, they absorbed new words.

I advise all the adopted parents I work with to monitor how their children are progressing with language and then how they do when they start school. Parents and pediatricians need to check in to make sure children are meeting appropriate milestones and markers. Language acquisition is the underpinning of how we learn.

That's why pediatricians always want to know how many words a young toddler can produce, how long sentences are, and other milestones. Yet those milestones are different for internationally adopted children, who are adjusting to a new language. The first part of this chapter covers how internationally adopted children make that transition. (Even if your child was not adopted internationally, you will find some useful suggestions about language development.)

I also discuss attention challenges in this chapter (specifically ADHD [attention-deficit/hyperactivity disorder]), because adopted children are more likely to be diagnosed as having these challenges. If your child is being screened for ADHD, please be sure to tell your pediatrician that your child is adopted because this fact may influence the diagnosis. A child exposed to trauma, illicit substances, alcohol, or other prenatal stresses may be at higher risk for developmental and behavioral concerns. In addition, symptoms of post-traumatic stress disorder or trauma can mimic or coexist with ADHD. I also describe sensory integration, a condition I have encountered in some adopted children in my practice.

What you need to know and remember is that learning and attention challenges usually do not exist in a vacuum. By that, I mean that it can be difficult to understand whether a language delay creates an attention challenge, or does the attention challenge make it hard to learn language? Is it a history of trauma or neglect that creates difficulties with learning to read, or does a child have dyslexia and an adverse early childhood history? What matters most, at the end of the day, is that your child receives appropriate evaluations, diagnoses, and ongoing support.

When your child is an infant and a toddler, your pediatrician is your first stop for questions about developmental delays and attention issues. As your child gets older, teachers and school psychologists will have insights, and their observations should be shared with your pediatrician to figure out next best steps. Always remember: You are your child's best and strongest advocate. Early referral is better than a wait-and-see approach.

Learning a New Language

Most internationally adopted children arrive home with early language delays, because they haven't experienced a language-rich environment in their native languages. If your child was in an orphanage, he most likely wasn't stimulated enough.

Then your child suddenly hears a new language and has to learn it. He switches languages when he gets home, yet another adjustment our children have to make. Of course, you provide a significant boost for your child by providing him with a language-rich environment. You are constantly talking to him, narrating events, and conversing. These constant interactions—even preverbal cooing back and forth—all help your child develop language. But as I said earlier, I'm amazed at how well—and how quickly—most children make this transition.

> "It is clear that adoption into a nurturing family improves children's language abilities."
> —*Sharon Glennen, PhD, CCC-SLP*

Child Care and Learning Language

I'm often asked whether a child should be placed into child care early (sooner rather than later) so he can be socialized and learn language quickly. I understand why you may think your child may benefit from being in a social situation, where he can learn how to interact with other children. But, if possible, it's best to keep your child with a caregiver or sitter as long as possible. That way, your child gets the one-on-one attention and personal interaction he needs to integrate the new language into his brain. If you have to go back to work and need to find child care, try to find a child care setting with a very low child to provider ratio. Toddlers don't learn language from other toddlers! They learn language from adults.

Research shows that, in general, the younger your child is when he is adopted, the quicker he will catch up. It's important to consider, though, how well he was learning his birth language before switching to English. If he had a solid understanding and use of his native language, it will be easier to learn English—even if he's a little older at the time of adoption.

Your child won't stay bilingual unless he has daily exposure to his native language. (Sometimes I see this if one adoptive parent speaks the native language or if siblings are adopted and both children continue to talk with each other in their native language). Otherwise, his birth language will disappear within 4 to 8 months. Then your child will be able to understand, and express himself, only in English. You will still need to pay attention for delays in vocabulary, comprehension, and reading.

Research supports what I encounter in my practice—children pick up English quickly and easily.[1] It's incredible how young children can learn so well and so fast. Regardless of the child's age, I typically see a marked improvement within the first 4 to 6 weeks home. Sometimes this improvement is an understanding of new language (receptive language), but often it's also an improvement in speaking (expressive language).

But remember that the standard guidelines for vocabulary acquisition or sentence length for all children don't apply to adopted children. Your pediatrician may ask you how many words your child says or how many words he strings together in a sentence. The expected number at certain ages may be higher than the number of words you've recorded. However, that difference does not necessarily indicate a problem, as your child has been home for only a short while. So that's why I want to give guidance, so you can factor in circumstances that your pediatrician might not consider when evaluating standard developmental milestones.

When to Be Concerned

As a pediatrician and a parent, I always tell the parents I meet with to *trust your instincts.* You know your child best. You know, day by day, how your child uses language. You know, week by week, whether he's improving or devising ways to get what he wants without saying it. You notice the minute improvements in pronunciation or vocabulary or in putting together sentences. Or, you notice when there aren't improvements. Not everything can be measured on a scale, so if you suspect something's going on, talk with your pediatrician.

I want you to pay attention to the following 3 aspects of language:

- Receptive language
- Expressive language
- Articulation

Receptive language describes your child's understanding of vocabulary. It's both what he hears and that he understands what you say to him, even if he can't respond with words.

Expressive language refers to word production—what words he uses and how he puts together sentences. Pediatricians generally evaluate kids with word counts, but that evaluation can be tricky with an adopted child. Language transition can make assessments difficult, and again, how quickly your child can bridge the gap depends on your child's age. It can be tricky to perform formal language screenings.

Articulation describes how speech sounds are made. If your child has trouble pronouncing sounds, your pediatrician should evaluate his hearing and might recommend a speech and language therapist for articulation issues.

I advise parents to start to worry when progression is *not* happening, which will be your subjective assessment. You will know what your child does or doesn't understand, even if he's not speaking many words. Your child might be babbling along and advancing, even though he hasn't uttered a word in English. Yet he can look at you, point to what he wants, or drag you to the refrigerator to get food. He can follow a 1- or 2-step direction such as "Bring me a book to read" or "Pick up the napkin and put it in the garbage, please." Doing so indicates that his receptive language skills are good—he understands what you are saying. And his babble or jargon demonstrates that he is getting closer to mastering words.

Robin remembers...

We had been home from China for less than a month when I took my daughter to a friend's house. She wandered around, exploring the toys, when my friend's mother offhandedly asked, "Honey, do you want to kiss your baby doll?" My daughter scooted back across the room and kissed the doll. My friend and her mother were impressed and surprised that she understood, considering how short a time she had been hearing English.

If you feel your child isn't progressing with either his receptive language or his expressive language, please talk with your pediatrician. I would rather families intervene earlier than later, even though there's a fine line between waiting too long and acting too early. Why not help your child if you can? Getting help for language skills certainly won't hurt your child.

If you suspect a speech or language delay, make sure your child has up-to-date hearing and vision screenings. Your child may have had middle-ear

"During the first year home, children adopted from abroad as infants and toddlers rapidly make the change from one language to another."
—*Sharon Glennen, PhD, CCC-SLP*

infections, which can lead to fluid buildup that can muffle hearing. You also never know when your child might need glasses. Adopted children are more likely to have vision disturbances. Robin was shocked to discover that her daughter at age 5 years needed a strong prescription, as she had been able to identify and name her letters with no problems during preschool. You also want to rule out other medical causes.

What to Expect Before Age 2 Years

If your child is adopted before 2 years of age, you should expect some sort of mild delay in his speech. For example, you may notice that he is behind his peers with vocalizations, gestures, or social interaction, which are all parts of preverbal communication. He might also be behind in symbolic play—understanding how to play with objects appropriately, such as pretending to talk on a phone and playing with toy kitchen utensils.

Language Development: What to Watch for in Your Child Before Age 2 Years

- How often does he make eye contact and try to communicate?
- What gestures does he make? A variety? With vocalizations? While gazing at you?
- How often are vocalizations? How varied? Have first words started?
- What kind of symbolic play? Pretend talking on the phone, putting stuffed animals to bed, or playing make-believe games?
- Able to comprehend new language? Simple commands and words?
- Ability to rhyme?
- Can your child carry a tune?

Keep in mind, though, that catching up is a process, which can take up to a year. Comprehension will usually develop before expression. Your child may be behind some of his peers.

If you feel the delays are more than mild or there's not enough improvement over time, I encourage you to have your child evaluated through early intervention (EI) services. A federal program funds an EI program in every state to offer services to children younger than 3 years with developmental delays. Ask your pediatrician about a referral to your local EI services. Early intervention providers will use standardized speech and language tests to evaluate your child. They will also ask for recent hearing and vision screening results.

What to Expect at Ages 3 to 5 Years

Children adopted at ages 3 to 5 years may have more-pronounced speech and language delays, and they will need more time to catch up. If at all possible, try to find out what you can about your child's pre-adoption speech and language development. Ask your child's former caregiver or foster parent, if available, how your child was doing (in his native—if relevant—language), as he may have had language delays already. Ask about expressive language: How long were his sentences? Did he use grammar and age-appropriate vocabulary? For receptive language, how did he understand questions or commands? How were his social interactions? Was he friendly or shy? Did he enjoy pretend play, interacting with others, and making eye contact?

> "Considering the pre-adoption environment and medical risk factors faced by these children, the fact that comprehension abilities emerge so rapidly is nothing less than incredible."
> —*Sharon Glennen, PhD, CCC-SLP*

It's also important to find out whether there were any articulation or pronunciation difficulties. Any sounds he had trouble making? Were there any difficulties with chewing or swallowing food?

Like younger kids, children aged 3 to 5 years are rapid learners. Comprehension can be a more reliable indicator of who needs EI services. Remember that expressive language—vocabulary and sentence production—takes longer for a child to master.

Language Development: What to Watch for in Your Child at Ages 3 to 5 Years

Consider interventions if

- Your child is not learning new vocabulary at a rapid rate.
- Your child is struggling with behavioral challenges. It may be that he struggles to understand what you say, or he can't "get the words out."
- Your child has regressed in any area of his development.

What to Expect at 5 Years and Older

Children who are adopted at 5 years and older are more likely to need immediate speech and language help and therapy. Your school-aged child will start school already behind and thus be at greater risk for falling even further behind in school. Your child's language gap will be much bigger, so it will take much more time to gain proficiency. Plus, consider all you need to know in English by elementary school! Reading may be a struggle, or your child might have difficulty with other subjects that involve reading, such as reading simple math problems or science facts.

If possible, try to find out whatever you can about your child's proficiency in his original language as well as about his schooling. Are any school records available? Is your child reading at, below, or above grade level? What about writing? What subjects are easy? Which are difficult? What is his attention span like? Can he work independently, or does he need help? Does he keep trying? Also, if possible, request an assessment in his native language as soon as possible to see whether your child has speech or language delays.

For a school-aged child, English as a second language classes may not be helpful if the child had language delays in his native language. English as a second language is useful for children and adults who have a strong foundation in their native languages. While English as a second language includes instruction in grammar, reading, vocabulary, and listening comprehension, its focus is to help people better their conversational skills. It is not designed to be remedial.

If your child starts understanding you quickly, he's probably doing fine and most likely will be fine when he starts kindergarten. However, keep in mind that classroom challenges may emerge, as

How to Help Your Child With Language Acquisition

- Read to your child regularly. Focus on reading material that is below grade level—even picture books are OK if they hold your child's interest.
- Take your child to the library. There, he can watch other children reading, and he can be exposed to a variety of book types—for example, storybooks, reference books, and nonfiction books.
- Be sure to limit screen time. Computer programs and video games do not enhance reading skills.
- Introduce music into your child's environment. (This advice doesn't mean Saturday piano master classes! Instead, I suggest playing music around the house, in the car, and anywhere so your child can start to enjoy the patterns in music and can listen for language in songs.)
- Ask for help from your child's teachers and special education teachers in your school district.

your child is using English in school before he is totally caught up. There's a risk for falling behind. You may want to arrange for speech and language therapy.

Other Language-Related Issues

Parents often ask me about other language difficulties that arise at different times in a child's development.

Stuttering

Parents sometimes worry when their toddlers and preschoolers stumble over their words or repeat words and phrases. I remind them that stuttering is typical for a newly verbal child. Remember how exciting it is for a child who is learning to talk—there's so much to say! Usually, these dysfluencies work themselves out. However, they occasionally lead to stuttering, when a child repeats sounds or syllables or prolongs sounds, such as "b-b-baby" or "sssssssometimes…." You might notice when your child has trouble making a sound; he might tap his hand or blink his eyes rapidly because he gets frustrated that he has trouble speaking clearly.

Your child may be at risk for stuttering if there's a family history of it, if he is a boy (more common in boys than in girls), if he has difficulties at age 4 years, or if he has other speech and language disorders. Stuttering is not uncommon, but if it persists for longer than 6 months, talk with your pediatrician about getting a speech and language evaluation and a recommendation for a certified speech-language pathologist. Children younger than 3 years can be evaluated through their local EI programs, while children older than 3 years can be evaluated through their school districts. You can also have a private evaluation.

The sooner someone can work with your child, the better. Your child can learn specific strategies and how to reduce tension and nervousness when speaking. You can also work with the therapist to learn how to indirectly help your child by changing how you communicate at home. It's good to talk with your child about stuttering, to be patient, and to minimize stressful situations that might trigger stuttering.

Selective Mutism

I have seen a number of internationally adopted children with selective mutism, which means your child chooses to speak only in specific settings and won't speak or has diminished speaking in other social situations. For example, at home your child will be verbal, but she will be silent in public or in the pediatrician's office. Selective mutism is easier to notice in older kids. Often, parents will show me video clips so I can hear and see their son talking in complete sentences at home but refusing to speak with strangers or at school. The difference is remarkable.

Selective mutism often occurs hand in hand with an anxiety disorder or extreme shyness. It often occurs in children who have been exposed to some type of trauma or neglect. Children often have difficulties in school as well, and it's difficult to know whether these school difficulties are related to speech challenges or are separate.

A child will be diagnosed as having selective mutism when the condition lasts more than a month and interferes with the child's success in school or wherever else he won't speak. It's important to obtain an accurate diagnosis and seek appropriate treatment from a skilled therapist. Using a low dose of a selective serotonin reuptake inhibitor can be helpful, and it is thought to reduce some of the anxiety.

Auditory Processing Disorder

I've met children who couldn't speak fluently or spoke in gobble-dygook. I needed to figure out why this challenge was happening. If you suspect your child is having similar challenges, you'll need to have your child tested by a skilled professional to figure out what's going on and how best to help him.

Auditory processing occurs when your child has trouble hearing sounds and can't understand the meaning of words. Background noise can make the situation worse because your child can't filter out or focus on what he is supposed to be listening to. This condition is usually diagnosed later, at about ages 7 to 8 years, by a trained audiologist. This condition may be linked to low birth weight or preterm birth, head trauma, chronic ear infections, or lead poisoning. A qualified speech and language therapist will know how to work with your child. The therapist will be able to provide suggestions to support your child in school. Your child may function best in a smaller, quieter learning environment. He may be able to use some reading technology; that is, he can have material read to him by a computer. The "reader" can read at a very slow pace, and your child can have the material repeated over and over until he masters it.

Starting School: Watching for Learning Differences

In the second half of first grade, the teacher called to say that Ethan was becoming more withdrawn in class, relying on his friend to help him figure out what to do. Other times, he was inattentive. At first, I thought that was fine—some kids are slower to learn to read than others are. But when the teacher called 6 weeks later and said his concerning behavior was continuing, I trusted her and realized I needed to get Ethan evaluated. I'm glad I didn't delay. The neuropsychologist did a full workup and discovered Ethan had a language-based learning disability. He wasn't goofing off or not trying; rather, he was having genuine difficulties learning. He needed to be in a smaller classroom with specialized teaching. He also needed language therapy for the basics of learning. Well, we started working with a speech-language pathologist immediately, and we all noticed a difference. Ethan became more confident in school, although he still struggled. I looked for a new school whose staff understood his learning style, and when he entered second grade, his learning took off as he was taught the way he needed to learn.

> — *Ben and Yael, parents to Ethan, adopted from foster care*

As I said earlier, all adopted children are at risk for language-based learning difficulties. Even if your child has caught up by kindergarten, difficulties can arise anytime. When you notice unusual behaviors, or if your child begins to get frustrated about school or doesn't want to go to school, consider having your child evaluated. The sooner you can help your child, the better it is for his learning, confidence, and self-esteem. If a child doesn't get basic concepts down, he will struggle with reading all his life. Be his strongest advocate and push for service, even if you are not certain your child needs it.

Learning difficulties can crop up in speech and language, as can problems with math, writing, and reading. As the American Academy of Pediatrics notes, "*Learning disorder* (LD) is a term used to describe a range of learning problems. These problems have to do with the way the brain gets, uses, stores, and sends out information. As many as 15% of children have an LD. An LD can appear at any point in time, not just when your child starts school. Many children find ways to work around their academic challenges, until, at some point, the school work becomes too hard. Children with LDs may have trouble with one or more of the following skills: reading, writing, listening, speaking, reasoning, and math. The most common type of LD is a reading disorder (dyslexia)."[2] Dyslexia is a receptive language-based learning disorder when a child has trouble with reading and understanding written words. Children with dyslexia have difficulties with processing language, decoding words, and reading comprehension.

Other learning disorders include

- **Dyscalculia:** A mathematically based learning disorder when a child has difficulty with understanding math concepts, solving math problems, or recalling math facts (such as multiplication tables and addition).

- **Dysgraphia:** A writing disorder when a child has a difficult time with handwriting, the hand-eye coordination needed, and the ability to write down what one is thinking.

Diagnosing learning disabilities requires an evaluation by a qualified professional, such as a psychologist, who will administer cognitive (IQ) and academic achievement tests. This can be done through your school district, or privately.

Seeing a Specialist

If you, or your school district, don't agree, or don't fully understand your child's learning profile, consider having your child evaluated by a neuropsychologist. A neuropsychologist conducts a more detailed evaluation that can identify your child's specific strengths and weaknesses regarding learning. What's helpful about this kind of evaluation is how thorough it is and how the neuropsychologist can tease out subtle ways your child's brain works differently. The evaluation can be extremely useful to you and your child, so you can all understand how your child learns best.

As part of a complete evaluation, the neuropsychologist will assess specific areas, such as

- **Executive function skills:** Planning, organizing, attention, and concentration.

- **Processing issues:** How your child processes information and gives output.

- **Memory and working memory:** How your child retains information or not in short-term memory as well as how quickly or not your child can remember stored information (what he has already learned).

- **Listening comprehension:** How your child hears and interprets the meaning of words.

- **Verbal expression:** How your child uses language to express himself.

- **Visual spatial processing:** How your child perceives objects in relationship to one another.

- **Visual motor processing:** How your child uses feedback from the eyes to coordinate movement of other parts of the body.

The evaluator will reach out to your child's teacher or observe your child in a classroom setting to see how he acts in a school environment.

Who May Be Working With Your Child if Your Child Has a Learning Challenge

Occupational therapist. Helps your child improve his motor, cognitive, sensory processing, communication, and play skills.

Speech and language therapist. Targets language-based learning disabilities and can also help with stuttering.

Learning specialist (at school). Focuses on specific areas of learning (reading, writing, and/or math) and works with your child's teachers to ensure that classroom instruction is as individualized as possible.

If your child is diagnosed as having a learning disorder, he will be eligible to receive educational intervention through your school district.

Attention-Deficit/Hyperactivity Disorder

More and more children are being diagnosed as having attention challenges, such as ADHD (attention-deficit/hyperactivity disorder). Depending on the source, estimates indicate that somewhere between 6% and 15% of school-aged children have some sort of attention challenge, with more boys diagnosed than girls are. The exact percentage of adopted children who have ADHD is unknown, but research suggests that it's more likely in this population. This developmental disorder and biologically based brain condition affects a child's behavior, attention, and learning.

Given the attention to ADHD, you are probably pretty familiar with the symptoms. For a child to be diagnosed as having ADHD, the symptoms should be present for at least 6 months, happen in various situations, and be more intense compared with behaviors of peers. The full criteria must have been met before age 12 years to receive a diagnosis of ADHD. Behavioral symptoms can be categorized into 3 groups—inattention, hyperactivity, and impulsivity. Here are some examples. Your child

- Has a hard time at school and in family or social situations
- May be impulsive or hyperactive
- Is easy to distract from work or play or has trouble concentrating
- Can be overexcited and find it difficult to sit still
- Has difficulty dealing with frustration
- Experiences mood swings
- May be inattentive—can't concentrate so daydreams or spaces out
- Often forgets things, seems careless, or is disorganized

Attention-deficit/hyperactivity disorder is not a learning disorder, although it can make it hard for a child to do well in school. Attention-deficit/hyperactivity disorder can coexist with learning disabilities, such as dyslexia, as well as mental health challenges such as anxiety and depression.

Whenever I screen a child for attention challenges, I always ask the parents about any trauma or stressful events their child may have experienced at any point. Make sure you share that information with your pediatrician too. Please know that symptoms of fetal alcohol spectrum disorder and post-traumatic stress disorder and trauma can mimic or overlap those of ADHD. Trauma can affect a child's working memory, inhibitory control, and cognitive flexibility.

Your pediatrician should be able to perform an initial screening test to assess for attention challenges and may ask you and your child's teachers to complete the NICHQ Vanderbilt Assessment Scales or the Connors Comprehensive Behavior Rating Scales. It's important to get information about how your child behaves in at least 2 settings, such as home and school. Your pediatrician, or referred provider (such as a psychologist), should be able to score these scales and make a diagnosis. Your pediatrician will also take a thorough history and perform a complete physical examination. She should check hearing and vision again, even if they've already been assessed. Your school district will not be able to make a diagnosis. If your child is diagnosed as having ADHD, only a physician will be able to prescribe medication. Stimulant medications are most commonly prescribed, along with age-appropriate therapy. You may also want to invest in some parenting courses to help you understand your child's behavior and help him with strategies. Many helpful resources are available.

It's Not Just Attention-Deficit/Hyperactivity Disorder

Most children with a diagnosis of ADHD have at least one coexisting condition. Please make sure your pediatrician considers *other* conditions that seem to be attention challenges.

These can include

- Learning difficulties that make it hard for your child to master specific skills such as reading and math.
- Oppositional defiant disorder or conduct disorder, which shows up in up to 35% of children with ADHD.[3] Children with oppositional defiant disorder tend to lose their tempers easily and annoy people on purpose, and they are defiant and hostile toward authority figures. Children with conduct disorder break rules, destroy property, get suspended or expelled from school, and violate the rights of other people. Studies show that this type of coexisting condition is more common among children with the primarily hyperactive and impulsive and combination types of ADHD. Your pediatrician may recommend behavioral therapy for your child if he has this condition.

- Mood disorders and depression, which affect about 18% of children with ADHD.[3] There may be a family history of these types of disorders. Coexisting mood disorders may put children at high risk for suicide, especially during the teenage years. If your child has a mood disorder or depression, your physician may prescribe additional medication that can work with a stimulant medication, and she may suggest therapy.

- Anxiety disorders, which affect about 25% of children with ADHD.[3] Children with anxiety disorders have extreme feelings of fear, worry, or panic that make it difficult to function. Your child may experience physical symptoms such as a racing pulse, chest tightness, sweating, diarrhea, and nausea. Counseling or different or additional medication (or a combination of counseling and medication) may be needed to treat these coexisting conditions.

- Language disorders. Children with ADHD may have difficulty with how they use language. A pragmatic language disorder may not show up with standard tests of language. A speech and language therapist can detect it by observing how a child uses language in his day-to-day activities.

- Post-traumatic stress disorder, as described in Chapter 7.

Sensory Integration Disorder

Sensory integration refers to the input we receive from our 5 senses and how our bodies respond to it. Some young children may seem extra sensitive or react strongly to loud sounds, strong smells, or the faintest touch, such as walking on sand or grass. Some children may have a poor sense of how their bodies should be positioned or moved in space and may have difficulty with balance or eye-hand coordination. Other children may rock or bang their heads to self-stimulate. These deficits are often described as *sensory deficits*.

Sometimes when children first join a family—either from international adoption or from foster care—they exhibit a lot of "crash and banging" behavior. They seem to run into everything on purpose or enjoy throwing themselves onto the ground. Sometimes they shovel food into their mouths. They are trying to regulate their senses by overstimulating themselves. Other children scream every time a parent brushes their hair or tries to trim their fingernails. They can be very particular about clothing material (eg, sweatpants only, no denim). They are overly sensitive to their environments. Most of these children benefit from specific therapy.

Sensory integration therapy is designed to help children cope with their sensory-processing difficulties and the resulting anxiety. Sensory integration therapy is typically performed by a pediatric occupational therapist with specific training or interest (or both) in this therapy. Therapy can be performed using a giant swing or a yoga ball; sometimes, jumping rope can help. The overly sensitive child can be helped by techniques such as brushing his body or gentle, slow exposure to whatever is bothersome (eg, the feel of new clothing). Through the therapy, a child learns to calm himself or reset his sensitivity "barometer." Most children learn to enjoy the therapy, and parents may be able to use the techniques at home. I've known children who ask to be brushed or know that it is time to "bounce on the ball" to help them calm themselves. Sensory integration therapy may be helpful for some children, even though there are still some questions about its scientific efficacy.

How to Talk With Your Child

You may not want to broach the topic of learning differences with your child. But it's easy to explain it in a straightforward fashion—everyone learns differently. Explain to your child that his brain is unique; there are some things his brain does very well, and there are other things his brain has a hard time doing. And you are going to help him understand how his brain works.

It is also helpful for families to understand that school may not be fun for your child. Let him know that you get that school is hard. But encourage him to think about school as his "job." And jobs, as we all know, aren't always easy or fun! Also, realize that your child can't always do his best. None of us can! So please pay attention to what your child tells you. Is he frustrated? Feeling stupid? Are things not going well? Is he forgetting to do homework? Or are there arguments and tears? Keep an open dialogue going with his teachers. Make sure that they understand his learning style and that he is getting the appropriate support.

If you start to see behavioral issues at school, always think about learning challenges as well as the possibility of bullying.

Helping Your Child

You are your child's best advocate. It's easiest for a child to learn in the situation that's right for him. Students who struggle in school can lose confidence and have decreased self-esteem. They may feel as if they are not as smart as their peers. Children learn in different ways, and they need to be in appropriate school settings to learn best.

Many more support options are available now. Often, schools—for whatever reason—cannot provide an environment that's conducive to a child's learning. Parents ask me about homeschooling. There are many advantages of homeschooling, but there are some disadvantages as well. It's a huge parental responsibility, and I've seen many families and children thrive after homeschooling starts. The disadvantages are that a child may feel socially isolated, he may not be able to get all the support services he needs, and parents need to own the educational process.

I want you to set your child up for success. There are many ways to learn the same thing, and sometimes, schools want to pigeonhole learners—and force square pegs into round holes. Your child doesn't need to be that person in the back of the class who is quiet or acting out or is anxious and depressed. Children don't intentionally misbehave. They are not inherently lazy. They want to be successful.

When a learning disorder or an attention challenge gets in the way, we can't change the child: we need to change the environment *around* the child. There's no shame or stigma in recognizing learning differences and taking steps for your child to learn in the best way for him. Children with learning differences may be more creative thinkers, may think out of the box, or may have artistic talent. Help your child know what makes him feel good about himself. You can do so by giving positive constructive feedback: "I like the way you use your hands to build things." "You really feel good about yourself when you can shoot baskets." Nurture his strengths.

Most important, try to help your child understand the way he learns best. Help him understand the way his brain is wired. "He learns best by having things read out loud to him." "She learns best by touching things with her hands." "He learns best when he's able to stand up, or move around, every 10 minutes."

Accepting Your Child for Who He Is

All the parents I know want their children to be happy and successful. I know it's hard to think that your child might have to take stimulant medication well into adulthood. But you may learn that your child functions better with medication. I know it's hard to imagine that your child might not be able to go to college. But college isn't necessarily the be-all and end-all for children. As parents, we have to alter our expectations from time to time, and that's OK. What's important is that our children grow up and can make meaningful contributions to society and live fulfilled lives. As parents, we have the opportunity to help our children make a difference by embracing who they are…just the way they are.

CHAPTER 9

Talking About Adoption

We are writing this chapter from our perspective as parents, as we both believe strongly in the all-important job of parents talking with their child openly and honestly about adoption as early as possible. You need to make time and space for discussions about your child's birth family, no matter how much you do or don't know about your child's birth parents. (Domestic adoptions may be open or closed; foster care adoptions or international adoptions may have varying levels of information about a birth family.) Talking openly about adoption leads to an increased understanding among family members and enhances the bond between children and parents. You don't want to have family secrets or to keep anything hidden.

That said, your discussions about adoption will vary over time. Children understand what adoption means in different ways at different ages and developmental stages. What your child understands as a preschooler differs from what she will emotionally and cognitively understand as a tween. No matter what your child's age, she needs to know you are willing to talk about her adoption.

As adoptive parents, our job is to keep the adoption conversation open, flowing, and supportive. And it is a *conversation*—not a lecture—between you and your child. Too often children are reluctant to bring up their feelings or questions for fear of hurting a parent emotionally or somehow disrupting the parent-child relationship. They may feel when they ask questions, they have to give up the family they have for the family they've lost. You can remind them that this isn't a black-and-white scenario. It's emotionally healthy for your child to yearn for her birth family, and you can encourage your child to have these feelings, acknowledge that

"[C]hildren's curiosity about their origins [is normal and] adoptive parents [should] validate and support their children's efforts to understand their pasts and find healthy connections to them."
—*David M. Brodzinsky, PhD*

she has them, *and* recognize the strong emotional connections she has to you!

You can be proactive by frequently talking about adoption. When your child accomplishes something, you might say, "I bet your birth mother would be so proud of you!" (If you have an open relationship, you could add, "Would you like to let her know about your success?"). On her birthday, you might mention, "I wonder if your birth mom is thinking about you today." These types of comments may help ease tough conversations.

Adoption raises difficult questions about loss, grief, and the following simple but devastating question: *Why didn't my birth parents want me?* Robin and I know that it's important to have ongoing conversations with our daughters in age-appropriate ways to match their emotional developmental stages. Yes, these conversations get harder as our daughters grow up, but they bring us closer and let our daughters know we are there to support their feelings.

When Your Child Asks Why You Adopted

Be prepared. At some point your child will ask: "Why did you adopt me?" She will want to know what motivated you. Maybe you always wanted to adopt. Perhaps conception was never an option, because of a medical reason, or you're single, or your partner is of the same sex. Maybe you experienced infertility. Whatever your story, I think it's important to be honest. Again, full disclosure is not required, depending on your child's age and emotional maturity, but honesty is the best policy. As your child gets older, she will wonder about infertility as she learns the various ways "babies are made." She may think she's second-best. This may be a hard, but necessary, conversation to have with her. As one mother told me, after years of infertility, "Once I made the decision to adopt, it felt totally right." That's important for a child to know.

How to Keep Your Child Talking With You About Adoption

Remember, adoption is part of who your child is. Throughout your child's life, there will be many opportunities to approach the subject of adoption. Many experiences with your family—for example, in your neighborhood, in your school community, in the media, and out in public—will offer material to bring to a discussion about adoption. One way you can encourage conversation is to make sure you surround your child with other adopted people. Having an adoption-friendly community outside your family will help your child feel as if she is not alone and will provide opportunities for her to talk about adoption with people who understand.

Think of weaving adoption language into your everyday conversations, whenever the timing seems right. Sometimes these conversations may occur spontaneously, when you least expect it. Often the period after tucking in and starting to fall asleep is a safe space when your child might express some of her more vulnerable feelings. It can be hard to muster the energy for an emotionally draining conversation at bedtime—you are tired too—but try as much as you can to be present for your child and to let her talk. Be open to listening to her. Please don't shut her down. If it's better to have a conversation at a different time, let your child know, explain why, and then follow up.

Another great time for a nonthreatening talk may be during a car ride, when your child is in the back seat and the conversational pressure is taken off. There's something about not staring into each other's eyes that makes starting a conversation easier. Many parents treasure the time they drive their children to activities or walk children to school.

Starting an Adoption Conversation

Here are some ways we have started a conversation with our daughters.

- What do you think adoption means?
- I wonder whether those children are adopted?
- What do you think your birth mother is like?
- Do you wonder about your siblings?
- Do you think you look more like your birth mother or your birth father? What makes you say that?
- What can you tell me about your adoption story?

Different Ages, Different Stages

Know that adoption conversations are going to take place throughout your child's life. Adoption is part of who your child is and how she became part of your family. Adoption doesn't end when your child joins your family. When talking about your child, some professionals, such as physicians and teachers, might use clinical language such as there's a "history of adoption" similar to how they might say there's a "history of prematurity." Family members, friends, or neighbors will often say that your child "was adopted," using the past tense. Perhaps they are thinking about the legal definition of *adoption,* which includes the process of termination of parental rights and finalization of adoption in court—when you've become your child's permanent, legal parents. But the reality is that your child "*is* adopted." Adoption is not a onetime event.

Telling Your Child She's Adopted

Parents often ask me whether they should tell their child she's adopted. Of course! It's essential to be completely honest with your child from day 1. That honesty doesn't mean you should share every detail right away. Use age-appropriate language when discussing your child's adoption story. You never want to surprise a child with details she is too young to understand. Experts suggest that parents disclose adoption details by the time a child is 12 years of age, right before puberty, which tends to be a pretty emotionally charged period of development. If the details are kept secret and disclosed during adolescence, a teen may have more difficulty with trust.

Remember that it's OK to say that you don't know something about your child's experiences. Don't make anything up. Doing so can be tricky, for example, when your child asks: "Do you think my birth mother loved me?" Our instinct is to respond: "Of course she did." Your child may perceive this response as somewhat dismissive. First, ask your child what *she* thinks. You might be surprised by the answer. And what your child thinks can help guide your response. You can also say something like "Your birth mother may have had to think very carefully about what would be best for you when she made your adoption plan. She may even have asked for help from other people—your birth father, family members, a social worker, a physician—about what would be best for you. So we know that she cared about you."

Now this response may be harder for a child to believe if she was removed from a home and placed in an institution or foster care. In these cases, a parent could say: "Being a parent is a big commitment. We think that your birth mother was not ready to be a parent. She lived in some tough circumstances. Maybe she didn't have a supportive family. Maybe she didn't have enough food or money to support her or a future family. Maybe she had some medical or mental health issues that made it hard for her to make good decisions about raising a child. We really don't know what her life was like. Not knowing is hard. And I know it's sad to think about your birth mother as having some personal problems."

As parents, we naturally want to soothe and reassure our children and make them feel better. We don't want them to feel hurt. Yet ascribing feelings to a birth parent or trying to wipe away the feelings your child has surrounding adoption may help in the short term but not in the long run as your child begins to understand what adoption means in a more sophisticated way. Robin and I remind ourselves that our daughters want the space to express their feelings and to be comforted. It's important to acknowledge that those feelings might hurt and be very painful.

Infant and Toddler Years: The What

Begin by talking very generally about babies and where babies come from. Yes, even at this age! You can find great picture books about baby animals. Then talk about how you became a family. Use adoption terms. Look at photos. Start using language about forming a family through adoption. Sometimes these conversations are more for you so you can become comfortable using adoption language. Your child will start to begin to understand her adoption story, the fact that she is adopted. There's no need for lots of details.

Preschool Years: The Why

Children aged 3 to 5 years begin absorbing parts of their adoption stories and may ask you to repeat the story over and over. Once a child enters preschool, you can expect that the concept of family will be part of the curriculum. Your child will start to notice similarities and differences about her peers' families. This awareness will be particularly true for adopted transracial families. Families need to acknowledge openly the racial differences that exist between their child and themselves. Parents can role-play with their children to help them develop appropriate responses with respect to any stereotypes. The same is true for same-sex adoptive parents. (I recall one adoptive parent telling me that everyone in her child's preschool class wanted "2 moms.") Some children will believe that adoption is the only way to make a family! There may be many questions about pregnant women and where babies come from. (I recall another adoptive parent telling me that her 4-year-old adopted son asked her whether she had breastfed him.) Some children may know that they were born in another state, or another country, but won't really understand what that means until they're older. (Another adoptive parent told me that her son thought that "all babies were born in Florida"!)

Children will pick up on the language you use, so be sure to use positive adoption language. Children this age are very egocentric— they want to talk about themselves, so we want to make sure they have accurate information. Keep in mind, however, that children this age make up a lot of stuff! It's developmentally normal for them to say things that aren't true. Your job is to help them keep their stories straight.

Positive Adoption Language

Consider using	*In place of*
Birth parent, parent	Real parent
Child who is adopted	Adoptee, unwanted child, given-away child
Is adopted	Was adopted
Child who joined his/her family through adoption	Chosen child
Make an adoption plan	Give up
Search, reunion, make contact	Track down, showed up on doorstep

Adapted from Adoption Network Cleveland's *Positive Language Guide.*

In addition to getting all the facts right, they will start to integrate all the different feelings they have about being adopted. Make sure your child understands that you are her family forever, and you will always care for and love her. Create positive feelings toward adoption. In addition to celebrating your child's birthday, you can celebrate her "adoption" day. You can also try to incorporate as much of your child's native culture or "before-adoption world" into your family. Introduce food, music, art, clothing, books, and anything that may be relevant.

Do remember, though, that most children this age still have limited understanding of what adoption means. (I have worked with a handful of preschoolers who have expressed grief and loss around their birth mothers. This grief is somewhat surprising, developmentally, but not impossible. Be sure to seek out a therapist who is comfortable working with children this age.) They really can't understand what adoption means. Keep the information short and factual. It can help to ask your child what she understands and knows. She might ask where babies come from—meaning a specific location—and not be asking for a detailed explanation of how babies are made.

School Years: The Details, Please

The school years are when a child's understanding of what adoption is, what it involves, and how and why it happens can change dramatically. Now is the time to explain more or ask what they are thinking. Follow your child's lead. This time is when a child might question why her parent "didn't want me" as she better understands her birth parents' circumstances or what options they had. It's healthy for children to be confused, angry, or hurt as they consider these questions. Know that your child's birth parents are always present, to some degree, in her mind.

During the school years, children gain a new understanding of the biological connections between family members. There's increased recognition of being biologically unrelated to the adoptive family and that a birth family exists. As one tween said, "You are not my real aunt; you are my adopted aunt." It's hard to process what it means to have 2 families.

Your child's birth family may or may not have some presence in your child's life. There may be cards and letters, or there may be connections through social media. Originally, you and your child may have had a very open relationship with her birth parents. You may live in the same community and see each other. As your child gets older, however, the frequency of contact sometimes diminishes. This shift can be extremely hard for your child and you. Remind your child that the adoption is probably not the reason this is happening. All families have some sort of instability, whether it's divorce or crazy "Uncle Joe." Family members come in and out of each other's lives. This fact may help normalize the experience with birth parents.

> "The struggle to understand and accept one's connection to 2 families, one of which may be unknown, fully emerges when children can conceptualize the nature of family in a more sophisticated way than when they were younger....[Children also] recognize that gaining a new family through adoption also means having been separated from a previous family."
> —*David M. Brodzinsky, PhD*

If possible, try to help your child maintain or establish some connections with members of her birth family. Recognize that she has other family members, besides her birth mother and birth father. She may have siblings, cousins, and grandparents. These family members may or may not want to know her. As her parent, you get to decide how much contact is appropriate. If you decide that contact is inappropriate, you need to be able to explain this decision to your child. Some parents tell their children, "Once you are 18, we believe you will be old enough to start making independent decisions about meeting members of your birth family and we will help you with this process, but right now you are a little too young." This boundary may confuse your child, and, for this reason, her desire for connection may become even stronger.

Let her know that you understand, and don't dismiss her yearning for connection. Her desire for contact *is* appropriate. This desire is the beginning of a lifelong process of establishing and maintaining healthy connections with her birth family. Again, this concept may scare you. You might wonder, *Will she leave me? Will she like members of her birth family better?* This situation is highly unlikely. All I'm suggesting is that it's important for your child to create connections. These are different from relationships. In this context, a *connection* means that your child has a link to others in her birth family and that birth family members are known. A *relationship* implies an ongoing interaction.

To help you understand, think of an internationally adopted child, who will, most likely, never have a relationship with any member of her birth family but can form connections when she visits her birth country and may travel to the community where she was born. Or, consider a child adopted from foster care, whose birth grandmother sends a birthday card every year, without fail. That's the only time you hear from her. There's a connection, not a relationship. A child who is adopted domestically as a newborn may know that her birth father liked to play basketball. She wants to play basketball like her birth father and fantasizes about playing basketball with him. That's a connection.

I've heard adopted children describe themselves as "split in 2" or that in their dreams they "fly back" to their birth mother and she greets them with open, loving arms. This time is when children may express more of their grief, either verbally or through behavior. Acknowledge these feelings and help your child talk about her sadness or anger—that she is sad she doesn't know her birth mother even though she wishes that you gave birth to her. How horribly confusing it is!

Children whose parents are of the same sex often say, "I wish I had a dad" or "I wish I had a mom." The reality is that they *do* have a father and a mother in either scenario—their birth parents! But it

Your Child's Search for Identity

We encourage you to show compassion around your child's expression of adoption-related losses. Even something as simple as a family-tree assignment or bringing baby pictures to school can be difficult for an adopted child. Birthdays and holidays can be tough as well. At Thanksgiving, when everyone sitting at the table is looking at everyone else, your child may be making mental comparisons: *Aunt Margaret has my mom's nose. My grandpa laughs like my dad. I'm not like anyone here.* Acknowledge and discuss physical differences and characteristics with your children. How do you honor birth parents around Mother's Day and Father's Day? Why might a birthday be difficult for your child? Again, be open to the questions, anger, and sadness. Speak with teachers and family members ahead of time, and make sure they understand the potential sensitivities around these events.

feels as if they don't. Again, there's lots of confusion and feelings to process.

It's crucial that your child understands that she did not cause the disruption or abandonment. What happened were adult choices that had nothing to do with her. But this reasoning is a hard thing to hear—many children harbor inside a feeling that somehow they are responsible for the adoption placement (like children feeling responsible when their parents decide to divorce). Some children with special health care needs may feel they were "abandoned" because they were "damaged" or "not loveable" owing to their medical conditions. Listen openly, and acknowledge and explore these feelings. You can't make them disappear.

Also, remember that it's very common for a child to fantasize about her birth parents and the alternate life she may have led. Ask

The Importance of Life Books

A life book is different from the photo album that documents your trip to meet your child. A life book compiles everything known about a child's history. It can help a child process all the thoughts and feelings about her adoption story and her life before becoming part of your family. These books are particularly useful for children adopted from foster care, who may have had several foster homes as well as important and meaningful relationships with others (eg, foster parents or siblings, other relatives, neighbors, teachers).

Consider making an ongoing life book that shows all the families that are a part of your child's life and connects her birth and adoptive families as one large extended family. A life book can be a work in progress, to which you and your child add information over time. It is a wonderful project to work on together. It's another way for children to express their feelings in a creative nonverbal fashion, with drawings and collages. Plus, it's a great excuse to go to the craft store to buy art supplies and stickers!

questions to figure out what she's thinking. "What do you think your parents were like? What would it be like to grow up in a different house, or a different country, and with brothers and sisters?"

When Your Child Says You're Not Her Real Parent

You may cringe when your child says, "I hate you. You're not my real mom (or dad, or parents)," but most children—adopted or biological—do, and this statement is emotionally healthy. Your adopted child may be beginning to acknowledge the truth about her origins. Getting to truth often starts with denial.

A child will fantasize about her birth parents and the alternate life she may have led. Ask questions to figure out what she's thinking.

"What do you think your parents were like? What would it be like to grow up in a different house, or a different country, and with brothers and sisters?" She may imagine her birth mother is a princess or that her birth father is a celebrity. And, these parents would be extremely permissive. No bedtime rules! Candy and ice cream for breakfast! These wishes can be strong, and the stronger they are, the more painful the reality of loss is for your child.

As painful as this stage is for everyone—you and your child—working through these feelings will help everyone in the long run. Your child's adoption story may be very complicated or it might be simple. Nevertheless, your child will have some underlying feeling of abandonment, a sense of loss. It's easy to lash out at you—and what child hasn't said hurtful words to their parents? It's difficult not to retort, but it's best to respond with love and understanding. Try to view this statement as an opener for talking about adoption—"It sounds like you wish you knew your birth mom"—or talking about the issue at hand—such as you not letting your child watch television at that moment. You can remind your child that parents are parents. A birth parent would most likely have the same rules—bedtime rules and no candy and ice cream for breakfast—as an adoptive parent does.

Teenagers: Separation and Identity Formation

Being an adolescent is hard enough! All teens struggle with issues of identity and how to separate from you. This search for identity leads adopted teens to intensely think about their birth parents. Many experience, for the first time, a true sense of grief and loss. They tell me that they "just don't fit in anywhere" and they "feel a deep emptiness inside." If you feel your child is suddenly anxious, or has slipped into a depression, consider that she may be wrestling with some of these feelings. Be sure to speak with your pediatrician or seek mental health consultation.

In addition to these tough, somewhat intangible feelings, your teen may start asking lots of questions, as she tries to figure out who she is. "Do you think my birth parents had (asthma, ADHD, learning differences, curly hair) like me?" No matter what she asks—serious or silly—the response could be something like "That's a great question. I bet you're curious about lots of things about your birth mother and family. It's hard not knowing the answers, and we may never know the answers for sure. Things like asthma, allergies, ADHD, and learning disorders tend to run in families. If one of your birth parents has ADHD or learning disorders, you're more likely, than someone whose birth parents do not, to have these things. That doesn't mean you're going to have these things for sure; it just means we need to keep this in mind."

> "Like all adolescents, adopted adolescents are in the process of trying to define themselves and find their place in the world. This process is more complicated for adopted individuals, however, because of their connection to 2 families, one that gave birth to them and one that is raising them. In their search for self, adopted teens must find a way of integrating aspects of both families into their emerging identity."
> —*David M. Brodzinsky, PhD*

Difficult Conversations

Some parts of your child's adoption story may be more difficult to discuss than others, such as if a child's birth mother or father has some present day challenges or had some troubles prior to the adoption. I've known kids who've asked their parents, "Do you think my birth mother used drugs or alcohol?" Again, honesty is the best policy. If you know, for sure, that her birth mother used drugs, then the answer is "Yes, she did." Wait for your child's response—she may be angry, or sad, or relieved.

Keep in mind that your child will want to love her birth parents. Always tell your child the truth, being careful to limit the amount and type of information according to the child's emotional and developmental ages. Help your child understand that all birth parents generally want the best for their children, but sometimes their actions or behaviors don't align with this desire. People may make poor choices or act irresponsibly, but doing so doesn't mean they are bad people. Create positive language around members of your child's birth family. Use their names, if they're known. "I know that your birth mom, Janea, loves music." Or, "Your birth father, Dan, is a good athlete."

If You Have Adopted From Foster Care

Keep in mind that many adoptions from foster care end up being adversarial between birth parents and adoptive parents, as birth parents often fight to keep their children. The courts decide otherwise and terminate their parental rights against their will. For this reason, establishing and maintaining openness with birth parents can be particularly challenging. You need to balance what you, personally, are comfortable with *and* what's in the best interest of your child. Like all parents, you will advocate for your child and protect her at the same time. Your child will have a very difficult time understanding the nuances of these situations, until she's much older. Working with a mental health professional can be extremely helpful for you and your child.

Searching for Family

At some point, your child may ask if she could search for members of her birth family. Hopefully, you've always supported openness around your child's adoption, which is why she's able to ask about a search. Remember, openness is important for all members of the adoption community. Many birth parents want openness too. They want secrets removed. It helps them with the grieving process, and they can experience a greater sense of self-determination. As adoptive parents, openness allows us to have greater empathy for all extended family members. But most important, openness for adopted children helps them be clear about who is parenting them, and it helps them with issues around pain and loss.

Searching can be complicated, but it is usually a healing experience during which all those involved can gain insight. Children are not the only ones who want to search; birth mothers often want to search for their children as well. Many years ago, birth records of adopted children were sealed in most states to protect birth mothers. Sometimes, adopted adults can secure a court order to gain access to their original birth certificates, but it's not always easy. Once they obtain the birth certificate, they may find that the birth mother redacted her name from the record. Courts want to protect the privacy of the birth mother also. Some states have established voluntary registries that can help connect birth mothers and adopted children. The good news is that more than 50% of the states in this country have opened access to birth certificates, and the number is growing.

Depending on the circumstances, a search could be simple or it could be next to impossible. Thanks to the Internet, searches are much more possible than they used to be. Nowadays, it's not uncommon for older children to attempt to search on their own, through social media. I've known domestically adopted teens who have found their birth mothers through Facebook. Some families return to their children's countries of birth and hire private services to search for birth connections. The possibilities are endless, but be prepared for the reality of missing information that will never be recovered. This reality can be really tough. While your child is a minor, it's up to you, as parents, to decide when the time is right and how best to support your child's wishes. Just because you find a birth parent does not mean a wonderful reunion will take place, but there can be all kinds of other, positive results from a search, including connections with birth siblings or birth grandparents, or maybe missing pieces of important family medical history. Most adopted individuals who decide to search are happy they did, regardless of the outcome. If your child wants to search, I suggest entering this process with guidance from a professional who is familiar with search options and the issues that might arise.

When You and Your Child Decide to Share Her Adoption Story

At different points in your child's life, she's going to decide to share her adoption story. We never know when this sharing is going to happen. Your child may be very comfortable disclosing details about herself and her parents. Conversely, she may be uncomfortable, and you'll need to check this feeling out with her. Know that her feelings will change throughout childhood. In general, my experience is that most children are pretty private about their adoptions for a number of different reasons, and these days, because families come in so many different shapes and sizes, people don't automatically assume a child is adopted. If your child happens to be the same race as you are, the fact that she's adopted may not be apparent at all. In this case, it can feel like a secret. Help your child know that there's a difference between keeping something secret and choosing not to share information because it's private. As a parent, it's your job to help her know when it's appropriate to share and that you, as the parent, may decide to share the information because it's important. For example, it may be relevant at a parent-teacher conference if your child is struggling in school: "We don't know whether her birth parents had learning disorders." If you and your child differ in race and someone questions whether you are her parent, you could answer: "I'm her mom (or dad)." You don't need to explain that she's adopted. If someone comments that your child looks "just like you," you could smile and say, "Yes, she's very good looking."

When these comments occur, I would talk with your child and check out how she feels about your response. At some point in her childhood, she may feel very proud that she's adopted and may want to tell everyone—even strangers—and if you don't acknowledge the adoption, your child may feel like you're lying. At other points, she may feel as if it's private information, and she may be confused about the right thing to say. Your job is to role model while taking cues from her.

Finding Support

No matter how old your child is, or her degree of interest in her adoption, it's good to know what resources are available in your community. You may be able to find outside support groups, school support groups, parent support groups, online chat boards, or affinity groups. A peer support group can be terrific—even though there may be a range of adoption stories, this group is a new way to make friends, and it's a safe space where your child isn't different because she's adopted. Think of support groups you may have attended—there's comfort in knowing you are not alone in your story. And there's often an easy shorthand with others who share the same experience.

A support group is a great place for parents to go to as well. You will typically find a supportive, caring environment where you can learn from each other. Robin and I have learned from adopted adults, who have shared their experiences and suggestions, as well as from our fellow adoptive parents. Most of us are new to this experience, so it's helpful to learn the best ways to support your child. Of course, it's not a one-size-fits-all experience. Families struggle with different issues. But it's helpful to hear those and consider how you might have handled a situation.

Ask your adoption agency for support group information. There may be local foster-parent groups or local chapters of international-adoption groups. It bears repeating that a qualified adoption therapist can help your child process difficult emotions around adoption or work with you and share advice on how to handle questions and situations.

The Conversation Continues

You will never know when the topic of adoption might pop up in conversation. And you will not necessarily know why your child asks a question or makes an adoption-related observation. Sometimes you will want to cry, sometimes you will want to give your child a hug, or sometimes you won't want to have the conversation. All those reactions are appropriate, and if you aren't prepared to talk at that moment, explain to your child that you need some time to consider what she said, and you will talk about it later. But please always remember to be honest at all times. This is such a personal and emotional topic for your child, and she wants to trust you with her feelings. Try to be there for her and listen. And please be patient and understanding with questions, or requests, to "tell me my story" over and over. As she gets older, she might also ask for more details about the circumstances of her adoption. Your conversation will continue throughout your child's life.

Epilogue

*A*doption has shaped both my professional life and my personal life. When I started caring for adopted children and children in foster care in the early 1990s, I had no idea that the practice of adoption medicine would become a specialty within the field of pediatrics. My passion for and interest in taking care of children who have been adopted have helped define my career as a medical professional, as well as who I am as a parent. Throughout my career, I have been surrounded by many people who have the same passion for taking care of adopted children, and I appreciate all that they have taught me. I am fortunate and grateful to have a job I love. I never think about my work as work.

When I first started the adoption practice in Albany, I really had no idea what to tell parents about the long-term outcome for their children. I remember thinking about the first adopted child I saw and wondering whether she was going to be OK. Her parents were asking me the same thing. I told them that we would figure it out together, and we would do whatever we needed to do to ensure that their child received optimal care. Now, 25 years later, I still say the same thing, but with a lot more confidence, based on a lot more experience.

My job as a pediatrician and an adoption medical specialist requires an investment in, and commitment to, lifelong learning—just like the "job" of being a parent. As parents, we are constantly learning, because we all want the best for our children. Robin and I hope that *Caring for Your Adopted Child* has helped you feel better prepared for what's to come. As I mentioned in the beginning of the book, you can prepare for only so much. The beauty of raising children is that as they grow, we grow too. Parenting makes us stretch our mental and emotional muscles. So what can we really prepare for? We can prepare to know that, as parents, we need to be flexible to meet our children's needs.

Most important, we hope that you now have a deeper appreciation and understanding of the unique aspects of what being adopted means—whether that means understanding the implications of early childhood experiences or the significance for your child of knowing—or not knowing—her biological family. And, unless you are adopted yourself, only your child truly knows how it feels to be adopted. Please honor and respect your child's perceptions and feelings. They belong to her, not you. Always listen carefully to what's spoken and what's left unsaid. This understanding will help you stay connected to your child.

No matter who your child is, we know that she is special to you and you love her more than she will ever be able to know. That's how we feel about our daughters. And we will always be grateful that our children helped us become who we are as people and parents and deepened our understanding of love and what makes a family. Adoption is now a part of all of us.

Resources and References

Resources

Adoptive Families [magazine]. New York, NY: Adoptive Families

Adoptive Families: The How-to-Adopt and Adoption Parenting Network Web site. https://www.adoptivefamilies.com. Accessed May 11, 2018

American Academy of Pediatrics. AAP schedule of well-child care visits. HealthyChildren.org. https://www.healthychildren.org/English/family-life/health-management/Pages/Well-Child-Care-A-Check-Up-for-Success.aspx. Updated June 27, 2017. Accessed May 11, 2018

American Academy of Pediatrics. Find a pediatrician or pediatric specialist. HealthyChildren.org. https://www.healthychildren.org/English/tips-tools/find-pediatrician/Pages/Pediatrician-Referral-Service.aspx. Accessed May 11, 2018

American Academy of Pediatrics. HealthyChildren.org. Accessed May 11, 2018

American Academy of Pediatrics. Healthy Foster Care America Web site. https://www.aap.org/fostercare. Accessed May 11, 2018

American Academy of Pediatrics Council on Foster Care, Adoption, and Kinship Care Web site. https://www.aap.org/en-us/about-the-aap/Committees-Councils-Sections/Council-on-Foster-Care-Adoption-Kinship/Pages/Foster-Care-Adoption-Kinship.aspx. Accessed May 11, 2018

Mason PW, Johnson DE, Albers Prock L, eds. *Adoption Medicine: Caring for Children and Families.* Elk Grove Village, IL: American Academy of Pediatrics; 2014

The National Children's Traumatic Stress Network (NCTSN). Families and caregivers. NCTSN Web site. https://www.nctsn.org/resources/audiences/parents-caregivers. Accessed May 11, 2018

Shelov SP, Remer Altmann T, eds. *Caring for Your Baby and Young Child: Birth to Age 5.* 6th ed. Elk Grove Village, IL: American Academy of Pediatrics; 2014

References

Introduction

1. Kreider RM, Lofquist DA. *Adopted Children and Stepchildren: 2010; Population Characteristics.* Washington, DC: US Census Bureau; 2014. Publication P20-575. https://www.census.gov/ prod/2014pubs/p20–572.pdf. Published April 2014. Accessed May 11, 2018

    See also Vandivere S, Malm K, Rade L. *Adoption USA: A Chartbook Based on the 2007 National Survey of Adoptive Parents.* Washington, DC: Office of the Assistant Secretary for Planning and Evaluation, US Dept of Health and Human Services; 2009. https://aspe.hhs.gov/hsp/09/NSAP/chartbook. Published November 1, 2009. Accessed May 11, 2018.

    See also Office of the Assistant Secretary for Planning and Evaluation (ASPE). The National Survey of Adoptive Parents (NSAP). ASPE Web site. http://aspe.hhs.gov/ hsp/09/NSAP/index.shtml. Published March 24, 2009. Accessed May 11, 2018.

2. Jones VF; American Academy of Pediatrics Committee on Early Childhood, Adoption, and Dependent Care. Comprehensive health evaluation of the newly adopted child. *Pediatrics.* 2012;129(1):e214–e223

3. Jones VF, Schulte EE; American Academy of Pediatrics Committee on Early Childhood and Council on Foster Care, Adoption, and Kinship Care. The pediatrician's role in supporting adoptive families. *Pediatrics.* 2012;130(4):e1040–e1049

4.   Vandivere S, Malm K, Radel L. *Adoption USA: A Chartbook Based on the 2007 National Survey of Adoptive Parents.* Washington, DC: Office of the Assistant Secretary for Planning and Evaluation, US Dept of Health and Human Services; 2009. https://aspe.hhs.gov/hsp/09/NSAP/ chartbook. Published November 1, 2009. Accessed May 11, 2018. Quoted by: Jones VF, Schulte EE; American Academy of Pediatrics Committee on Early Childhood and Council on Foster Care, Adoption, and Kinship Care. The pediatrician's role in supporting adoptive families. *Pediatrics.* 2012;130(4):e1040–e1049

5.   US Department of State Bureau of Consular Affairs, Intercountry Adoption, Web site. https://travel.state.gov/ content/travel/en/Intercountry-Adoption/adopt_ref/adop-tion-statistics.html. Accessed May 11, 2018

6.   Jones J, Pacek P. National adoption data assembled by National Council For Adoption. In: Johnson C, Lestino M, eds. *Adoption by the Numbers: A Comprehensive Report of U.S. Adoption Statistics.* Alexandria, VA: National Council For Adoption; 2017:1–10. http://www.adoptioncouncil.org/ publications/2017/02/adoption-by-the-numbers. Published February 15, 2017. Accessed May 11, 2018

7.   Adoption and Foster Care Analysis Reporting System (AFCARS). FY 2016 data. Administration for Children and Families Web site. https://www.acf.hhs.gov/sites/default/files/ cb/afcarsreport24.pdf. Published October 20, 2017. Accessed June 25, 2018

8.   Table 17. In: Johnson C, Lestino M, eds. *Adoption by the Numbers: A Comprehensive Report of U.S. Adoption Statistics.* Alexandria, VA: National Council For Adoption; 2017:52–53. http://www.adoptioncouncil.org/publications/2017/02/ adoption-by-the-numbers. Published February 15, 2017. Accessed May 11, 2018

Chapter 4

1. Foli KJ, Thompson JR. *The Post-adoption Blues: Overcoming the Unforeseen Challenges of Adoption.* New York, NY: Rodale; 2004

2. Senecky Y, Agassi H, Inbar D, et al. Post-adoption depression among adoptive mothers. *J Affect Disord.* 2009; 115(1–2):62–68

    See also Foli KJ, South SC, Lim E, Jarnecke A. Post-adoption depression: parental classes of depressive symptoms across time. *J Affect Disord.* 2016;200:293–302.

3. Foli KJ, Gibson GC. Sad adoptive dads: parental depression in the post-adoption period. *Int J Mens Health.* 2011;10(2):153–162

Chapter 5

1. Coles CD. Prenatal substance exposure: alcohol and other substances—implications for adoption. In: Mason PW, Johnson DE, Albers Prock L, eds. *Adoption Medicine: Caring for Children and Adolescents.* Elk Grove Village, IL: American Academy of Pediatrics; 2014:97–122

2. McQueen K, Murphy-Oikonen J. Neonatal abstinence syndrome. *N Engl J Med.* 2016;375(25):2468–2479

3. National Institute on Drug Abuse. *Dramatic Increases in Maternal Opioid Use and Neonatal Abstinence Syndrome.* Washington, DC: National Institute on Drug Abuse, National Institutes of Health, US Dept of Health and Human Services. https://www.drugabuse.gov/related-topics/trends-statistics/infographics/dramatic-increases-in-maternal-opioid-use-neonatal-abstinence-syndrome. Updated September 2015. Accessed May 11, 2018

4. American Academy of Pediatrics. Caring for babies born with cleft lip and/or palate: AAP report explained. HealthyChildren.org. https://www.healthychildren.org/ English/health-issues/conditions/Cleft-Craniofacial/Pages/ Cleft-Lip-and-Palate-Parent-FAQs.aspx. Updated April 24, 2017. Accessed May 11, 2018

5. American Academy of Pediatrics. Spina bifida. HealthyChildren.org. https://www.healthychildren.org/ English/health-issues/conditions/developmental-disabilities/ Pages/Spina-Bifida.aspx. Updated November 11, 2015. Accessed May 11, 2018

Chapter 7

1. American Academy of Pediatrics, Dave Thomas Foundation for Adoption. *Helping Foster and Adoptive Families Cope With Trauma.* Elk Grove Village, IL: American Academy of Pediatrics; 2015

2. American Psychiatric Association. *Diagnostic and Statistical Manual of Mental Disorders.* 5th ed. Washington, DC: American Psychiatric Association; 2013

3. Keyes MA, Malone SM, Sharma A, Iacono WG, McGue M. Risk of suicide attempt in adopted and nonadopted offspring. *Pediatrics.* 2013;132(4):639–646

4. Slap G, Goodman E, Huang B. Adoption as a risk factor for attempted suicide during adolescence. *Pediatrics.* 2001;108(2):1–8

Chapter 8

1. Glennen S. New arrivals: speech and language assessment for internationally adopted infants and toddlers within the first months home. *Semin Speech Lang.* 2005;26(1):10–21

2.   American Academy of Pediatrics. Learning disabilities: what parents need to know. HealthyChildren.org. https://www.healthychildren.org/English/health-issues/conditions/learning-disabilities/Pages/Learning-Disabilities-What-Parents-Need-To-Know.aspx. Updated November 21, 2015. Accessed May 11, 2018

3.   American Academy of Pediatrics. Common coexisting conditions in children with ADHD. HealthyChildren.org. https://www.healthychildren.org/English/health-issues/conditions/adhd/Pages/Identifying-Coexisting-Conditions.aspx. Updated January 9, 2017. Accessed May 11, 2018

Index

A

AAP. *See* American Academy of Pediatrics (AAP)

ADA. *See* American Dental Association (ADA)

ADHD. *See* Attention-deficit/hyperactivity disorder (ADHD)

Adolescence
attachment issues in, 117–118
separation and identity formation in, 183–184
suicide in, 140–141
watching for mental health issues in, 139–140

Adoption
domestic, xxiv–xxvi, xxviii, 39–43, 72, 85, 87, 107, 125–126, 145
from foster care (*See* Foster care, adoption from)
international, xxiv–xxviii, xxx, 26, 39, 42–43, 48, 52, 87, 145–148
open, 5–6, 171
parents' questions about, 5–9
pediatrician consultation before, 3–5
post-traumatic stress disorder and, 134–135
statistics on, xxiv–xxvi
talking about (*See* Talking about adoption)
traveling for, 6–7

Adoption medicine, 193
Adoption therapists, 126–127, 138
Age and attachment, 106
Alcohol exposure. *See* Fetal alcohol syndrome (FAS)
Alvarado, Susan Branco, 103
Ambivalent attachment, 113–114
Amblyopia, 95
American Academy of Pediatrics (AAP)
adoption medical specialists, 3
on childhood trauma, 125, 139
on circumcision, 55
growth charts by, 44
on health supervision visits, 82
HealthyChildren.org Web site, 85
on laboratory tests, 46
parenting books by, 19
on positive parenting, 137
on post-adoption evaluation, 39
on post-traumatic stress disorder, 132
on prenatal exposure to substances, 86

American Cleft Palate-Craniofacial Association, 85
American Dental Association (ADA), 54
American Psychiatric Association, 120

Anxiety
about eating, 67
ADHD and, 164
attachment, parents', 118–119
managing your child's, 76
selective mutism and, 156
separation, 76, 77

ARC. *See* Attachment, self-regulation, and competency (ARC)

Articulation, 149

Attachment, 103–104
age and, 106
ambivalent, 113–114
challenges with, 105–108
disorganized, 115–116
disruptive behavior and, 108–110
indiscriminate social behavior and, 111–113
issues in later years with, 117–118
meaning of, 104–105
parents' anxiety about, 118–119
patterns of, 110–118
personality and temperament and, 108
placements and, 106–107
promoting healthy, 107
reactive attachment disorder (RAD), 119–121
strengthening over time, 121

V

Vaccinations and immunizations,
    48–49, 62, 64
Verbal expression, 160
Vision problems, 95–96
Vision screening, 53
Visual motor processing, 160
Visual spatial processing, 160

W

Well-child visits, 82, 126
Working memory, 160